songbird

FABULOUS FEMALE VOCALISTS FROM BILLIE HOLIDAY TO BRITNEY SPEARS

DONALD F. REUTER

UNIVERSE

NINA SIMONE AT THE VILLAGE GATE

This book is dedicated to my great friend Kevyn, and other enlightened souls, who love the "sound" of women in music.

on the cover: Beautiful **Lena Horne** (b. 6/30/17, Brooklyn, N.Y.) is the epitome of *Songbird*. She endured everything from having her skin lightened for her first MGM film appearance (*Panama Hattie*, 1942) to seeing her musical numbers removed from films for distribution in the Deep South and being blacklisted in the fifties. But, she emerged triumphant with the 1981 one-woman show, *Lena Horne: The Lady and Her Music*, which won her a Tony and two Grammys. (publicity still from the film *Til the Clouds Roll By*, 1944. Everett)

front endpaper, from left to right: The **McGuire Sisters** (Chris, b. 7/30/29; Dorothy, b. 2/13/30; and Phyllis, b. 2/14/31, all Middletown, Ohio), seen here with **Anna Maria Alberghetti** (*second from left,* b. 5/15/36, Pisaro, Italy), blended the novelty of sisterhood with precise harmony in the hits "Sugartime," "Sincerely," and "May You Always." A pixie-ish Alberghetti won a 1961 Tony Award for her lead role in *Carnival* (a remake of the 1953 film *Lili*) and starred in *Cinderfella* (1960) with Jerry Lewis, but she is probably best known to recent audiences as a salad-dressing spokesperson. "Delicioso!" (candid of McGuire Sisters and Alberghetti, c. 1958. Leaf/Michael Ochs Archives)

frontispiece: Long before her role as "Carol Brady" ("mother of three very lovely girls") in the long-running TV series *The Brady Bunch* brought her fame, **Florence Henderson** (b. 2/14/34, Dale, Ind.) starred in the Broadway musical *Fanny* (1954), among others; was a semi-regular on *The Jack Paar Show*; sang and did the weather as the "*Today Show* Girl" during the late fifties and early sixties; and was the first female guest host of *The Tonight Show*. (Everett)

title page: **Kathryn Grayson** (b. Zelma Kathryn Hedrick, 2/9/22, Winston-Salem, N.C.) was one of filmdom's most beloved singers. During the forties and early fifties, her light soprano could be heard in a number of great movie musicals, including the classics *Anchors Aweigh* (1945), *Showboat* (1951), and *Kiss Me Kate* (1953). She is seen here with her daughter, Patti-Kate. (Corbis)

this spread, from left to right: A trio of contemporary music's most popular and outspoken talents: **Mary J. Blige** (b. 1/11/71, Atlanta, Ga.) brought back low-down blues with a hip-hop groove; the minx in mink, **Li'l Kim** (b. Kimberly Jones, 6/11/75, Brooklyn, N.Y.), is the sauciest singer since Eartha Kitt; and **Missy "Misdemeanor" Elliott** (b. Portsmouth, Va.) takes the "rap" for being R&B's biggest, baddest mama. (Michael Thompson)

inset: Arguably, jazz great **Nina Simone** (b. Eunice Waymon, 2/21/33, Tryon, N.C.) could have been a far bigger success if she had cared to compromise her beliefs. But she never has. You can feel some of her forcefulness in the 1959 recording of "I Loves You Porgy" (from Gershwin's *Porgy and Bess*) and in the mesmerizing "I Put a Spell on You" (also the title of her autobiography). (album, *Nina Simone at the Village Gate*, Colpix, 1962)

First published in the United States of America in 2001 by **UNIVERSE PUBLISHING** A Division of Rizzoli International Publications, Inc. 300 Park Avenue South New York, New York 10010

Designed by Donald F. Reuter

Printed in Singapore

2001 2002 2003 2004 2005 2006
10 9 8 7 6 5 4 3 2 1

Library of Congress Control Number: 2001089983

contents

this spread: In spite of her brother's failed attempts to follow in their famous father's footsteps, **Nancy Sinatra** (b. 6/8/40, Jersey City, N.J.) had a recording career that moved along a decidedly more upward path. Her hits included "These Boots Are Made for Walking" (1966), a pop ditty that can still get 'em on their feet, and the mildly controversial duet with her dad, "Something Stupid." (Why controversial? A father and daughter singing lyrics together was felt to be slightly incestuous; regardless, the song still went to number one!) During the sixties, Sinatra was married to teen heartthrob Tommy Sands (could you imagine Frank as your father-in-law?); appeared in a number of films, including *Speedway* (1966) with Elvis Presley; and had her own Emmy-winning special, the trippy *Movin' with Nancy* (1968). (candid of Sinatra at home, 1967. David Sutton/MPTV)

inset: It's easy not to take the career of **Eydie Gormé** (b. 8/16/31, New York City) and her husband Steve Lawrence seriously, but the couple's contribution to entertainment goes far beyond late-night comedy lampoons. Gormé sang with dance bands before she became a regular on Steve Allen's *Tonight Show* (working along with her soon-to-be hubby). Soon after, the twosome moved up the ladder of success. Gormé had a number of top-40 hits, including "Blame It on the Bossa Nova"—incidentally, Gormé speaks and sings in fluent Spanish—and a 1966 Grammy win for her version of Jerry Herman's "If He Walked into My Life" from the musical *Mame*. (That same year, she just happened to beat out Nancy Sinatra's "Boots"!) Husband and wife shared a Grammy as 1960's best vocal group for "We Got Us" and an Emmy for the television special *Steve and Eydie Celebrate Irving Berlin* (1978). (album, *Eydie Gormé*, ABC-Paramount, 1957)

Eydie Gormé

a stroll down melody lane

Stop! in the name of love . . . for female singers. If you think you've found the definitive document on women in music, put this book back where you found it. With easily a thousand artists who could be included and room for only a hundred or so, how could this book be definitive? (My humblest apologies go to those ladies who could not be squeezed in!) You're probably thinking how audacious it is of me to even attempt such a treacherous undertaking, knowing full well the possibility that the absence of many of your favorites could incite a riot. Nevertheless, the deed is done, and *Songbird* is a tribute to *all* the talented ladies (included or not) who, through song, made the world a more harmonious place to live in—and listen to.

As a gay man, I have always had a particular fascination with the subject of women in music. There is a long-held belief that gay men and female vocalists (in general) are some-how inextricably connected. Culturally, gay men have been linked with every great female singer of the last one hundred years. I know I have always felt a greater emotional kinship with the dames and not the dudes of music. Why? First of all, a gay man thinks he is afforded a certain amount of dramatic hyperbole with which to rule his life, and as we all know exces-sive feeling is supposed to be a feminine trait. Women, unhindered by a straight-male ego, allow themselves to express unbridled emotion in music. Therefore, with what may be seen as exceptionally sentimental songs, the two groups are brought togeth-er. Whether accompanied by a disco beat ("At first I was afraid, I was petrified") or violin strings ("Oh, my man I love him so, he'll never know"), this type of music could be directed only to another woman or a sissy.

Another reason behind the connection is the fact that many gay men lead a sort of Peter Pan existence, which provides the opportunity to enjoy a greater range of music. We tend to be able to appreciate songs that would be deemed either too young or too old by others in the listening audience. Happily, this way we can delight in Britney Spears, Madonna, Eartha Kitt, *and* Sarah Vaughan, all at the same time, without any of the guilt or pressure to loosen up or grow up that others might feel. Of course, these theories could all be taken as gross generalizations. For instance, if straight men stopped buying records, Janet Jackson and Mariah Carey would have to take on second jobs to make ends meet. However, I do think gay men understand—a little better than straight men—where a woman's heart is when she expresses her hurt and longing—especially when an errant male is to blame!

---

this spread: "The Florida Thrush," **Frances Langford** (b. 4/4/14, Lakeland, Fla.), was a radio and musical feature star, but it was her association with Bob Hope and his famed USO tours that forever cast Langford as the dedicated, selfless entertainer of our men in uniform. (In fact, Langford was instrumental in convincing Hope to undertake this venture.) Langford was once married to actor Jon Hall; owned her own nightclub; and has a visitor center—devoted to ocean marine life—named in her honor along the Florida coastline. (publicity still, 1935, Everett)

inset: Almost singlehandedly, pretty little **Deanna Durbin** (b. Edna Mae Durbin, 1921, Win-nipeg, Canada) saved her movie studio, Universal, from going under. Considered a rival talent to Judy Garland, Durbin's gooey-sweet personality and singing worked like a snake charm on unsuspecting audiences. (But, brother, bring along a shot of insulin to get you down off of this high.) (78 rpm record set, *Deanna Durbin*, Decca, 1940)

But now to a less personal take on the subject: The "herstory" of music is a tale of talent, ambition, and most of all, survival. For much of civilization, women were allowed to be little more than "chorus girls" for the compositions that men wrote, produced, and orchestrated. Even at the beginning of the twentieth century with the invention of sound recording, females were seen, but very infrequently heard. On rare occasions, a lady would be given the spotlight, and sometimes, like the once very popular Lillian Russell, become a major star. (Men would even prefer to sing songs intended for a female's voice rather than let a woman do the honors. We can be such scoundrels!) All that would start to change with women's emancipation and a more modern point of view during the jazziest age of them all—the twenties. The music industry, though still dominated by men, loosened up considerably and a number of women such as Bessie Smith found careers that allowed them at least a small measure of financial and spiritual independence. Unfortunately, the decade that saw women given the right to vote and the rise of Afrocentric music also saw the instigation of Prohibition and the looming shadow of the Great Depression.

In the thirties, women stepped back into the home, allowing men to take the only available jobs. Radio became a popular source of *free* entertainment. Film, however, was entering into its golden age, and musicals, the shiniest of them all, attracted droves of weary patrons eager to pay for one night of lovely music from Grace Moore or Jeanette MacDonald. Then the war came, and our boys went overseas. Big bands, which had risen to great popularity in recent years via the swing movement, placed gorgeous girl singers, like Helen Forrest and Margaret Whiting, in front to ostensibly boost morale. This period also saw female vocalists choosing to go solo with greater frequency than ever before.

By the fifties, general prosperity also brought about the first truly idyllic time for women in music; the convergence of jazz, soul, pop, and country music styles resulted in a boon of talented female vocalists. Women were queens of the charts. The biggest single of the decade was Patti Page's "Tennessee Waltz." But a little incoming thing called rock and roll quickly put an end to that dance. During the sixties, women remained popular—Connie Francis, The Supremes, etc.—but men owned rock music and regained their places as kings of the music industry.

Nevertheless, by the late sixties and early seventies, a cultural morass had taken over the country and women's voices could again be heard—in protest *and* song. The singer/songwriter (Carole King and Joni Mitchell are some notable examples)

----

this spread: You might be under the impression that the increased popularity of Latin music in recent years was the first such occurrence, but that impression would be mistaken. Music, as in all forms of entertainment, works in cycles. Years before Jennifer Lopez (or would that be J-Lo?) sambaed her famed derriere to the top of the charts, **Carmen Miranda** (b. Maria do Carmo Miranda Da Cunha, 2/9/09, Marco de Canavezes, Portugal; d. 8/5/55) was an even bigger hit wearing hats piled high with fruit and six-inch platform heels. In many a Technicolor musical, she stole the show from her hapless costars and for a time became the highest-paid performer in the world. (Kobal)

inset: **Gloria Estefan** (b. Gloria Fajardo, 9/1/57, Havana, Cuba), who once worked as an interpreter at the Miami airport and was studying psychology just prior to her move into recording, has remained a key figure in music since she and her Miami Sound Machine first spiced up the airwaves in the mid-eighties with "Conga" and "Bad Boy." (Carolyn Gangi/Retna)

became the scribe of the day, and "me generation" music lovers got a potent case of Saturday night fever when temperatures were raised by a large injection of disco divas. By decade's end, thanks to Donna Summer and other dancing queens, women held their ground.

The eighties saw the birth of the music superstar, and no one sang her way faster to the top than Madonna. However, the divine M's ascent was seen as both a blessing and a curse to the recording industry. At this point many artists (and producers) became more focused on the packaging of the product rather than its content. But Ms. Ciccone's appearance laid the ground-work for a near-complete female domination of the music scene by the last decade of the twentieth century.

In the nineties, women were having their say—and the variety of voices doing the talking was delightfully overwhelming. From pop-music juggernauts Janet Jackson and Mariah Carey (the decade's number-one artist) to soulful stylists Whitney Houston and Toni Braxton; from the laid-back laments of Sarah MacLachlan and Shawn Colvin to the ribald rockin' of Alanis Morrisette and Sheryl Crow, sisters were doin' it for themselves. The future for women in music? Things look and sound brighter than ever before; keep your ears tuned.

Finally, I'd like to offer a few notes on how *Songbird* was put together. In this book, you will *not* find clearly defined separations between the different categories of music. The beauty of music is that it has no real boundaries, and the free-flowing narrative of *Songbird*—which alternately feels like waltz and a rhumba—reflects this perspective. The contents of *Songbird* also do not follow a specific order from greater to lesser or from older to younger. However, there is a unifying beat—think of it in melodic terms—that connects the passage of one genre into another, and one individual to the next. Most women in *Songbird* are paired with a fellow singer. Sometimes, the connection between the two is obvious; often, it is subtle. The photographs in *Songbird* are accompanied with vintage album covers, sheet music, and magazines from my private collection. These were chosen specifically to add visual interest; in no way are they representative of the artists' best (or worst) work. I do, however, frequently mention a specific song or album in the text; these are merely personal recommendations. (Look for more suggestions at the back of the book.)

That's it! *Songbird* will undoubtedly hit chords both sharp and flat, high and low, but hope-fully, all of it will keep you singing.

inset: In 1992, after a duo of amazingly successful LPs, **Janet Jackson** (b. 5/16/66, Gary, Ind.) signed the largest single-artist recording contract in history—for fifty million dollars. (Ironically, it was surpassed by her brother Michael's own deal within a week.) Jackson is a gifted interpreter of music's most satisfying new sound; a blend of old- and new-school styles, it is a unique one-world tribal sound that you can dance to. (album, *Janet*, Virgin, 1992)

this spread: As a high-school student, **Lauryn Hill** (b. 5/25/75, South Orange, N.J.) was voted homecoming queen, which must have been a portent of good things to come. She was a series regular on the daytime soap *As The World Turns* before her group, The Fugees, became one of the most successful rap acts of the nineties. Her 1998 solo effort *The Miseducation of Lauryn Hill* nabbed her a record five Grammys in one evening, including Best New Artist. (candid of Hill in 1997. Duncan Raban/Retna)

13

make mine music

Daughter of a tailor and a mezzo soprano, **Dame Joan Sutherland** (b. 11/7/26, Point Piper, Australia) had her opera debut at Covent Garden in 1952. However, it was after her marriage to pianist Richard Bonynge in 1954 that her career came to prominence. Under his "guidance," she began taking on roles that helped her perfect her talent. By 1959, she was an operatic star with a lauded performance in *Lucia di Lammermoor*. After her debut in 1961 at La Scala in Italy and the Metropolitan in New York, she was affectionately dubbed "La Stupenda." She was given the title "Dame" in 1979. Sutherland officially retired in 1990. (candid of Sutherland making up for her role as Lucia di Lammermoor, backstage at Covent Garden, London, 1961. Hulton Getty/Archive)

this spread: As a little girl, famed American soprano **Leontyne Price** (b. Mary Violet Leontyne Price, 2/10/27, Laurel, Miss.) received a toy piano. From that moment on she was, in her own words, "center stage." Price went to school at Julliard in New York City and worked her way to the opera stage first via Broadway—chosen by Ira Gershwin himself, to play Bess in a 1952 revival of *Porgy and Bess.* She then went on to television in NBC's triumphant 1955 production of *Tosca* and made her Metropolitan debut in 1961. In 1966 (as Cleopatra in the original work *Antony and Cleopatra*) she opened the Met's new building at Lincoln Center. Retiring in 1985 with a performance of *Aida,* Price is the recipient of the Presidential Medal of Freedom and an astounding thirteen Grammy Awards (though she lost her initial race for Best New Artist of 1960—if you can imagine!—to comedian Bob Newhart). (portrait, 1957. Gene Howard/MPTV)

inset: During the seventies, the invigorated popularity of opera in America owed a great deal to **Beverly Sills** (b. Belle Miriam Silverman, 5/25/29, Brooklyn, N.Y.)—and I count myself as one *partial* convert. In a field famous for diva-like behavior, her quite likeable personality (how could she not be with the nickname "Bubbles"?) and talent brought arias and librettos to a larger audience. But can you imagine established patrons squirming in their velvet seats at the thought of this coloratura soprano performing with Carol Burnett and the Muppets? (You could expect nothing less from a girl who started singing at age three on the radio show *Uncle Bob's Rainbow House!*) From 1979 to 1989, Sills made news by becoming the first woman director of the New York City Opera—bringing it back to financial solvency—and in 1993 became the first woman to chair New York City's Lincoln Center for the Performing Arts. (Sills's Metropolitan Opera debut was in 1975; her age, forty-six.) (portrait of Sills, 1969. Hulton Getty/Archive)

inset: **Anna Moffo** (b. 6/27/32, Wayne, Pa.) had her unofficial singing debut at the tender age of seven, singing for a school assembly. As a teen, her talent and beauty attracted the attention of Hollywood. However, Moffo declined Tinseltown's call (for the time being) and went on to study voice in Rome (where she once worked as an x-ray technician!). Her official singing debut was at Spoleto in 1955; soon after she appeared at La Scala. Her Metropolitan debut was in 1959. During the early sixties, Moffo was voted (by Italians) as one of the world's most beautiful women. Twice married, Moffo's second husband was former RCA chairman Robert Sarnoff. (album, *One Night of Love*, RCA-Victor, 1965)

this spread: **Maria Callas** (b. Cecilia Sophia Anne Maria Kalegeropoulos, 12/2/23, New York City; d. 9/16/77) moved with her mother back to their homeland, Greece, where her life in opera commenced. However, her return to New York was when the legend truly began: she turned down her first two roles for the Metropolitan—Fidelio and Madame Butterfly—although the venue itself cites an unfavorable audition; a trip to Venice jump-started her career when she was given the lead in an opera when the original star had taken ill; at this time, the late forties, she married a man thirty years her senior, Giovanni Meneghini. In 1950 she replaced Renata Tibaldi in *Aida* at La Scala, becoming a sensation, and in 1955 she was sued by a former manager for $300,000. One year later Callas made her Metropolitan debut at the precise moment that *Time* magazine published a scathing interview with "La Divina's" mother (with whom she was no longer speaking). However, she received sixteen curtain calls at the end of her performance. Parting company with Meneghini in 1959, she began her nine-year love affair with Aristotle Onassis, whom she fully expected to marry but who instead wed Jacqueline Kennedy. By the mid-sixties Callas's voice was losing its power and numerous performances were canceled or performed with disastrous results. In 1969, she made the film Pasolini's *Medea*, which received tepid reviews. By the early seventies, drugs entered her life, and she was once on the verge of death by an accidental (though some say intentional) overdose. In 1973, Callas embarked on a world tour for the first time in eight years. Its final stop was Sapporo, Japan, in 1974; this audience would be the last to hear her perform in person; finally, falling ill one morning in 1977, she died before medical attention could reach her. (candid, Callas leaving La Scala in 1958 after a dispute with management. Hulton Getty/Archive)

this spread: Many of us know **Marian Anderson** (b. 2/27/1897, Philadelphia; d. 4/8/93) as the black woman who sang on the steps of the Lincoln Memorial in the spring of 1939—by arrangement with then–First Lady Eleanor Roosevelt. Originally, she was set to appear at Constitution Hall. However, the building's owners, the Daughters of the American Revolution, would not allow a person of color to perform on the premises. Because Anderson was a major personality, the controversy shed a harsh spotlight on the abhorrent practices of the time. However, this was hardly the first instance that Anderson suffered from racial discrimination: she had been denied admission to her first choice for a music school because of her color, and early in her career had found it necessary to move to Europe in pursuit of gainful employment. Even when she triumphantly returned to the states, she found herself unable to stay, dine, or enjoy company at the places where she appeared—despite being a box-office draw. At the age of fifty-seven, Anderson was asked to perform as the first African American on the stage of the Metropolitan Opera. Though her voice was not in peak form (and there were other, younger talents available), no other personality could do justice to this monumental occasion. Arturo Toscanini called hers "a voice that one hears once in a hundred years." A suggested musical selection is "Nobody Knows the Trouble I've Seen." (TimePix)

inset: It's rather fitting that **Kate Smith** (b. 5/1/07, Washington, D.C.; d. 6/17/86) was born in the nation's capital, since she would eventually become one of the country's favorite daughters. A popular radio star, Smith's robust figure certainly didn't stop her from appearing in a number of films and in her own hit television shows. But her "biggest" claim to fame came when she recorded Irving Berlin's "God Bless America" (which he considered his most important composition). A rousing bit of political propaganda—which can be seen and heard in the wartime pic *This Is the Army* (1943)—it is one of recorded music's most successful, enduring, and recognizable pieces. Fittingly, the last time Smith sang the tune in public was for the nation's bicentennial in 1976. (album, *Kate Smith,* Capitol, 1997)

KATE SMITH

21

sweet inspirations

Though her place as gospel music's premier artist is as solid as the "rock of ages," it is not too surprising (given the tenure of the times for black performers) that early in her career **Mahalia Jackson** (b. 10/26/11, New Orleans, La.; d. 1/27/72) worked as a domestic and learned the skills of beautician—just in case things didn't work out! Among the highlights of her life: being asked to sing before Dr. Martin Luther King's historic "I Have a Dream" speech in Washington, D.C., in 1963; a performance at John F. Kennedy's inaugural ball in 1960; her own CBS radio show in the fifties; and her recordings for Columbia records—all of which helped bring her work to the white mainstream (though she was considered "the only Negro whom Negroes made famous" by the early African-American press). Despite attempts by others to have her record secular music, Jackson remained resilient though she well understood the connection among church music, R&B, and rock and roll. In keeping with that sentiment, Jackson was inducted into the Rock and Roll Hall of Fame in 2001. She also won three Grammy awards, including one awarded posthumously in 1976. A popular recording is "Move on Up a Little Higher." (candid of Jackson, c. 1956. Richard Miller/MPTV)

inset: Hailed as the "queen of American folksingers," both Joan Baez and Bob Dylan credit **Odetta** (b. Odetta Holmes Felious Gorden, 12/31/30, Birmingham, Ala.) with influencing their own careers. Starting out as a classically trained vocalist, Odetta turned to "ballads and blues" in the mid-fifties. These dark yet soulful works, sung in her magnificently deep and throaty voice, along with her imposing physicality, made a compelling combination indeed. Eventually, Odetta recorded more traditional, though no less memorable, pieces of folk music and spirituals ("Sometimes I Feel Like a Motherless Child") and immense popularity followed her into the sixties—as did the careers of many notable folksingers. But when the immediacy of the genre fell out of public favor, her career (and those of others) faded. Nevertheless, Odetta continues to perform today, and rarely can one hear a voice of such intensity and power, mixed with such intimacy and gentleness. (album, *Odetta at Town Hall*, Vanguard, 1962)

this spread: **Miriam Makeba** (b. Zensi Miriam Makeba, 3/4/32, Johannesburg, South Africa) first came to prominence in the late fifties as a jazz vocalist with the group the Manhattan Brothers. By the early sixties, she had gone solo, eager to bring her unique voice to the world. In 1960, Makeba was nominated for a Grammy as Best New Artist; the same year she was exiled from her homeland (and not allowed to return for thirty years). Becoming a "citizen of the world," she spoke out against the evils of apartheid and other forms of racism. Often referred to as "Mama Africa," she was the first African (*not* African American) performer to win a Grammy. Her "Pata Pata" was a top-10 hit in 1967. She also has the dubious distinction of having sung at JFK's 1962 birthday party (you know, the same event where Marilyn appeared!). Still performing today, on occasion with Odetta, Makeba has had a career that is a testament to the resilient power of music. (portrait of Makeba, 1960. Maurice Seymour/MPTV)

sister to sister

this spread: Though today they are regarded as music giants, **Gladys Knight** (b. 5/28/44, Atlanta, Ga.), and her omnipresent Pips (whose name was purloined from a manager's nickname) worked for years to gain a foothold on the ladder of success. Forming way back in 1952, the group was considered a second-string act until the release of "I Heard It through the Grapevine" in 1967. Then Knight's gutsy vocals on "If I Were Your Woman" (1971)—one of Motown's biggest-selling singles—solidified her own place among top female vocalists. By that time the group was also moving away from their original bluesy sound—and Motown—to something more MOR (middle-of-the-road), which explains why they were alternatively perceived as a pop or R&B group. The decision proved quite fortuitous and made the seventies a more harmonious place with a string of classics, including "Neither One of Us" (a Grammy winner), "Midnight Train to Georgia" (another Grammy winner and their only number-one pop hit), and "The Best Thing That Ever Happened to Me." Gladys and her Pips were all related, but that would not stop the group from separating in the late seventies. They reunited for a few years and collected another Grammy but split for good in 1989. The group became inductees into the Rock and Roll Hall of Fame in 1996. (Michael Ochs Archives)

inset: Officially dubbed the "Queen of Soul" (how do these "titles" actually become official?), **Aretha Franklin** (b. 3/25/42, Memphis, Tenn.) has enjoyed a lengthy ride at the top. With fifteen Grammys to her credit, she is also the music industry's most-honored female. Early gospel recordings reflected an upbringing at the hands of a well-to-do reverend father and tutelage from none other than Mahalia Jackson. Ironically, her second label, Columbia, tried to position Franklin as a black torch singer—the idea did not take. A switch to Atlantic in the mid-sixties liberated her talent: Franklin's recordings of "Think," "Respect," and "Natural Woman" still pack a wallop today—well over thirty years later. Unfortunately, although her work is still highly regarded, recent releases have little of the spark that once set the world on fire. But look out for her long-awaited venture into opera—coming soon. (Michael Ochs Archives)

Chaka Khan (b. Yvette Marie Steven, 3/23/53, Great Lakes, Mich.) was christened with the name Chaka at age thirteen by an African shaman (the surname "Khan" come from a brief marriage). In 1971, when she was just eighteen, she hooked up with the fledgling band Ask Rufus (quickly shortened to Rufus) and set about to revolutionize rock, pop, and soul music. Khan's sexually-charged vocal delivery brought the group their first major hit, "Tell Me Something Good" (1974)—written especially for Khan by Stevie Wonder—and their first Grammy. A second statuette, for "Ain't Nobody" in 1983, came when Khan was already considered a solo artist. Her 1984 smash "I Feel for You," a mesmerizing blend of R&B, dance, and rap written by Prince, also won a Grammy. Surprisingly, Khan is also an award-winning actress—for her London stage role in *Mama I Want to Sing*—and a purveyor of confectionary delights: she manufactures a line of chocolates under the name "Chakalates," the proceeds of which she donates to charity. Isn't that a "Sweet Thing"? (Michael Ochs Archives) *this spread:* **Roberta Flack** (b. 2/10/39, Asheville, N.C.). Defining Flack's career is harder to do than it looks. Because she is black, many simply perceive her as an R&B/soul performer. But look closely at where her biggest hits enjoyed equal chart time, and she falls into the area of pop. Add to the equation what some consider a leaning toward jazz, and you begin to see the dilemma. However, it's likely that Flack finds the whole idea of categorization abhorrent—as well she should. Flack's first smash (after two decades of trying) was "The First Time Ever I Saw Your Face." Though recorded a few years earlier, including it in the film soundtrack for *Play Misty for Me* (1971) brought it almost instantaneous recognition and subsequently, Grammy awards for Record and Song of the Year. Flack followed with two more Grammy-winning songs, "Where Is the Love?"—a duet with frequent partner Donny Hathaway—and "Killing Me Softly with His Song." (portrait of Flack, 1969. Hulton Getty/Archive)

inset: Though her raspy voice has often been compared to Billie Holiday's and Nina Simone's, as a child **Macy Gray** (b. Natalie McIntyre, 1970, Canton, Ohio) hardly spoke at all. She thought she sounded funny and kept to herself, earning a reputation for being shy. (Years later, she even believed record executives were kidding when they reacted positively to her demo tapes.) Her unique style of music is the result of a deep love for singers like Stevie Wonder and going to a nearly all-white boarding school where the attendees listened only to rock music on the radio. As a songwriter, the message on her stunning 1999 debut album, *On How Life Is,* may be quite personal, but cuts like "I Try" have universal appeal. (candid of Gray, 1999. Youri Lenquette/Retna)

birds of a feather

this spread: Before the formidable trio of **LaBelle** (*left to right:* Nona Hendryx, b. 8/8/45, Trenton, N.J.; Sarah Dash, b. 8/18/43, Trenton, N.J.; Patti LaBelle, b. Patricia Holt, 5/24/44, Philadelphia) had their ultra-racy 1974 hit "Lady Marmalade," (which was remade in 2001 by Christina Aguilera, Li'l Kim, Mya, and Pink) they were a quartet billed as the Blue Belles. (Incidentally, an original member, Cindy Birdsong, left the group in 1967 to replace Florence Ballard in the Supremes.) For years, the group struggled valiantly to only middling success. They held on long enough to cross over from the sixties into the seventies— something the majority of all-female groups were not able to do—and emerged as a far more forceful entity. Together, with sexually suggestive lyrics (that's an understatement!) and a brazen sense of visuals—to this day their costuming is unparalleled—LaBelle had finally arrived. Unfortunately, their dance with fame lasted only a few moments; Hendryx left in 1976, and the group quickly folded. Subsequent solo releases by all members were met with some critical, if not always commercial, success. Founder Patti LaBelle is the only member who has gone on to greater accolades. (candid of LaBelle in performance, c. 1976. Michael Putland/Retna)

inset: Possibly the coolest, sexiest, and *craziest* trio in music, **TLC** (*left to right:* Tionne "T-Boz" Watkins, b. 4/26/70, Des Moines, Iowa; Rozonda "Chilli" Thomas, b. 2/27/71, Atlanta, Ga.; Lisa "Left Eye" Lopes, b. 5/27/71, Philadelphia) started out with a funky edge ("Ain't 2 Proud 2 Beg") that mutated into a slick, sophisticated sound ("Creep") within the span of a couple years. With these hits, and many others, TLC became the most successful female group since the Supremes. But such near-instantaneous fame and fortune were not without a (much-publicized) downside: Lopes, in a rage, burned down the house of her pro-football boyfriend, Andre Rison, was arrested, and then checked into rehab. Despite sales in the multimillions, the group declared bankruptcy due to mismanagement of funds. Their 1999 album, *FanMail*, reinforced their reputations as urban contemporary feminists with the hit songs "No Scrubs" and "Unpretty." Ever the visual pioneers, too, they express themselves vividly in person and on film (as in the 1995 award-winning video "Waterfalls" from the *CrazySexyCool* album). (John Kelly/Retna)

this spread: The **Supremes** (*left to right:* Florence Ballard, b. 6/30/43, Detroit, Mich.; Mary Wilson, b. 3/6/44, Greensville, Mich.; Diana Ross, b. Diane Earle, 3/26/44, Detroit, Mich.) first recorded as the Primettes in 1959, but it was not until their chart-topping success with "Where Did Our Love Go?" in 1964 that they became the darlings of the music world. During their reign as the Queens of Motown, the group was also the top-selling singing act of the sixties— just behind the Beatles! Their entire list of hits (including eleven number ones) would be far too long to reprint here, but more than a few—including "Stop! In the Name of Love" and "Someday We'll Be Together"—are bona-fide pop classics. Unfortunately, the honeymoon did not last forever. Composers Holland-Dozier-Holland continued to write after the much-publicized 1969 breakup, and the Supremes kept recording without the delectable Ms. Ross, but the group's stay on top came to an end. However, the brief success of the Supremes goes far beyond their lyrical legacy and occupies a very special place in music history: at a time when racial barriers were still very much in place, this trio of African-American women were the first to unapologetically use their sex appeal to successfully cross over—and dominate—white mainstream charts. No small feat, and a door opener for the innumerable ethnic (as well as nonethnic) female groups to follow. (candid of Supremes in performance on the set of *Hullabaloo*, 1965. George Joseph/MPTV)

inset: Often compared to the Supremes, **Destiny's Child** (*left to right:* Kelly Rowland, Beyoncé Knowles, Michelle Williams) has already weathered some of the same ups and downs as their famed predecessors— most notably the departure of two founding members, the replacement of one member during their breakout year, and a landslide of attention (à la Diana Ross) focused on beauteous Knowles. Hits like "Say My Name" have garnered lots of attention for the group (named after a chapter in the Book of Isaiah), but whether they have the "Survivor" skills to become legendary along the same lines as the lovely trio from Detroit remains to be seen—and heard. (candid of Destiny's Child, 2001. Stonehouse/Camera Press/Retna)

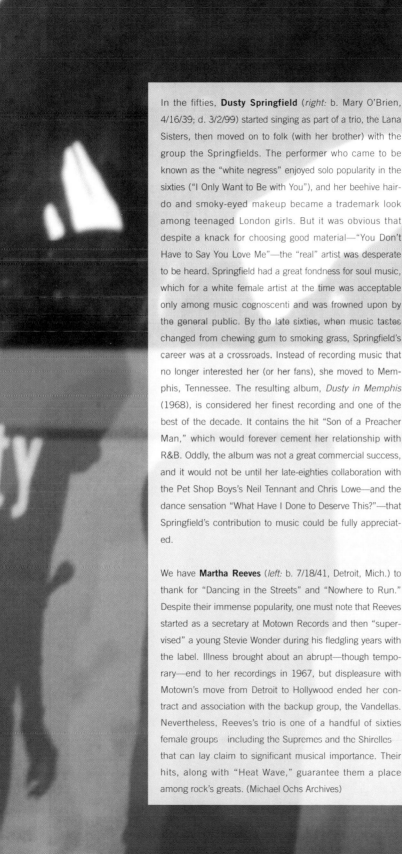

In the fifties, **Dusty Springfield** (*right:* b. Mary O'Brien, 4/16/39; d. 3/2/99) started singing as part of a trio, the Lana Sisters, then moved on to folk (with her brother) with the group the Springfields. The performer who came to be known as the "white negress" enjoyed solo popularity in the sixties ("I Only Want to Be with You"), and her beehive hair-do and smoky-eyed makeup became a trademark look among teenaged London girls. But it was obvious that despite a knack for choosing good material—"You Don't Have to Say You Love Me"—the "real" artist was desperate to be heard. Springfield had a great fondness for soul music, which for a white female artist at the time was acceptable only among music cognoscenti and was frowned upon by the general public. By the late sixties, when music tastes changed from chewing gum to smoking grass, Springfield's career was at a crossroads. Instead of recording music that no longer interested her (or her fans), she moved to Memphis, Tennessee. The resulting album, *Dusty in Memphis* (1968), is considered her finest recording and one of the best of the decade. It contains the hit "Son of a Preacher Man," which would forever cement her relationship with R&B. Oddly, the album was not a great commercial success, and it would not be until her late-eighties collaboration with the Pet Shop Boys's Neil Tennant and Chris Lowe—and the dance sensation "What Have I Done to Deserve This?"—that Springfield's contribution to music could be fully appreciated.

We have **Martha Reeves** (*left:* b. 7/18/41, Detroit, Mich.) to thank for "Dancing in the Streets" and "Nowhere to Run." Despite their immense popularity, one must note that Reeves started as a secretary at Motown Records and then "supervised" a young Stevie Wonder during his fledgling years with the label. Illness brought about an abrupt—though temporary—end to her recordings in 1967, but displeasure with Motown's move from Detroit to Hollywood ended her contract and association with the backup group, the Vandellas. Nevertheless, Reeves's trio is one of a handful of sixties female groups including the Supremes and the Shirelles that can lay claim to significant musical importance. Their hits, along with "Heat Wave," guarantee them a place among rock's greats. (Michael Ochs Archives)

this spread: At age fifteen, **Stephanie Mills** (b. 3/26/56, Brooklyn, N.Y.) eased on down the road to fame when she was given the star role in the Broadway musical *The Wiz.* By then she was already a seasoned performer: it was her second show; and years before she had won, for six weeks in a row, the acclaimed talent contest given at the famed Apollo Theatre. (Despite her success playing Dorothy, Mills lost the role to Diana Ross for the hugely budgeted film version.) A tiny powerhouse of a singer, Mills signed with Motown after her Broadway run, but the association was short lived; her hits came when she went with 20th Century, and songs such as "Never Knew Love Like This Before" were great chart successes. However, her performance of "Home" (from *The Wiz*) stands out as her signature work. Listening to it you can easily understand why it was considered such a shame when she was passed over for the film role in favor of "box-office appeal" (incidentally, the part had to be rewritten—and aged—for Ms. Ross). However, Mills may have gotten the last laugh: the picture was a flop. (Michael Ochs Archives)

inset: White singer **Teena Marie** (b. Mary Christine Brockert, 3/5/56, Santa Monica, Calif.) not only started out and thrived in soul music, but her whole career took advantage of the novelty. (Remarkably, no photos of Marie appear on her first album; Motown execs were afraid people wouldn't buy it if they knew she was white!) Her professional and personal relationship with funkmeister Rick James greatly influenced Marie's work, especially cuts like "Square Biz" and "Behind the Groove." Unfortunately, Marie's relationship with Motown was just the opposite: she sued the label in 1982 for unpaid royalties. Based on the court's ruling in Marie's favor, a law called the Teena Marie Bill was passed by the U.S. Congress to protect artists' money. As a songwriter, "the Ivory Queen of Soul" has written a number of nicknames—"Lady T," "Li'l bit," and "Casper"—into the lyrics of her songs, but Marie's first hit, "I'm a Sucker for Your Love," was written by James and was originally intended for Diana Ross. (Michael Ochs Archives)

this spread: For being one of the most beloved and vilified of all female singers, **Diana Ross** (b. Diane Earle, 3/26/44, Detroit, Mich.) is truly without peer—though her exact contribution to the music industry (and pop culture) is difficult to articulate. Because success came quickly and in large part from white audiences, Ross was often perceived as turning her back on her race, and because she had great success on the pop charts, her work was easily dismissed as pandering to popular tastes. The reality is that a great deal of Ross's output—both as a Supreme (see page 35) and a soloist—is far more rooted in classic R&B (and was skillfully written, orchestrated, and produced) than it has ever been given credit. One can argue the main reason for all the brouhaha was that Ross was both black *and* breathtakingly beautiful, which in a world fast giving the external more importance than the internal, made for a potent (and timely) combination. Of course, much attention has also been given to the "diva" aspects of Ross's appearance and behavior. But her larger-than-life personality gives legions of fans a great deal of satisfaction—and let's not forget that Ross's captivating presence may have single-handedly broken down color barriers. Quite an accomplishment for the little girl from Detroit's Brewster Projects. Her biggest solo hit: "Upside Down." Her best loved song is a toss up: I vote for "Love Hangover" (because with it you get a slow and a fast song!) An Oscar nominee for Best Actress in *Lady Sings the Blues* (1972), Ross has *never* won a Grammy. (candid of Ross in performance on the set of the Hollywood Palace, 1968. Sheedy&Long/MPTV)

inset: **Monica** (b. Monica Arnold, 10/24/80, Atlanta, Ga.) wasn't even born when "Upside Down" was a hit (yikes, doesn't that make your head spin?!), but like everything else nowadays, she squeezed a helluva lot into the last twenty years and, out of the recent group of female R&B artists (which includes singer Brandy, with whom Monica had the smash duet "The Boy Is Mine"), ended up becoming the most successful. Because of her extreme youth—at fourteen she was the youngest person to top the Hot 100 (with "Boy")—she had a full-time tutor as part of her entourage. For one so young (and beautiful), she is a surprisingly mature and caring individual (I speak from firsthand knowledge), and we can all look forward to what her future brings. (portrait of Monica, 2000. Lucy Fitter/Retna)

41

and all that jazz

this spread: Thankfully, the tragic (and triumphant) story of **Billie Holiday** (b. 4/7/15, Baltimore, Md.; d. 7/17/59) has not faded from memory. To encapsulate: as a child, Holiday was raped and then placed in an institution; as a teen, she became a prostitute. Scared to death of recording, she did it only because it kept her from "whoring." In the late thirties, she toured with Count Basie and Artie Shaw (who became a lover). Then, Holiday went solo but was ill equipped to manage herself properly—both professionally *and* personally. An addiction to heroin and alcohol, together with a succession of relationships involving abusive men, triggered a steady decline in her work. By the mid-forties, after being arrested for drug use, she "dried out" (but never got over the feeling that fans came to see her only to look at the scars on her arms). Unfortunately, the "cure" was temporary; she went back into a sanatarium in 1952. She sang constantly, but was out of step with fifties jazz and lacked the musical knowledge to make the sound work for her limited vocal range. By the late fifties, she had been refused permission to adopt, so she lived alone with her dog. In 1959, when Holiday lay dying in the hospital, she was arrested for drug possession. All this, not too mention the horrific racism she had to endure, makes listening to "Strange Fruit," "Lover Man," and "T'ain't Nobody's Business" a very poignant musical experience, indeed. (candid of Holiday performing onstage at the Sugar Hill nightclub in Newark, N.J., 1957. Hulton Getty/Archive)

inset: By contrast, **Ella Fitzgerald** (b. 4/25/17, Newport News, Va.; d. 6/15/96) seemed to live a charmed life. Her career started almost by chance: winning an amateur night contest at Harlem's Apollo Theatre in 1934 led to a first singing job. Beginning with the hit "A-Tisket, A-Tasket" (which she co-wrote based on the nursery rhyme), Fitzgerald's upbeat, crystal-clear voice and personal charm won the hearts of millions, eventually earning her the title "America's First Lady of Song." Though a preeminent jazz "scat" artist, Fitzgerald's greatest musical contribution was in the category of popular standards. Over the course of many years, she recorded her "songbook" series, which in most cases created the definitive version of works composed by the twentieth century's greatest songwriters (Rodgers & Hart, Gershwin, Johnny Mercer, Duke Ellington, Cole Porter, et al.). (Michael Ochs Archives)

this spread: Many people are only familiar with **Della Reese** (b. Delloreese Patricia Early, 7/6/31, Detroit. Mich.) as one of the stars of the television drama, *Touched by an Angel.* Actually, it was her heaven-sent voice that, over forty years ago, first caught the public's attention. Her 1959 smash "Don't You Know" was a striking example of what beautiful things can be created when elements from two vastly different areas of music are masterfully combined: specifically, a work of opera ("Musetta's Waltz" from Puccini's *La Boheme*), rewritten with English lyrics, and most compellingly, Reese's powerful, soulful singing. A killer. (portrait of Reese, 1955. Maurice Seymour/MPTV)

inset: Of the twentieth century's most important female singers, **Dinah Washington** (b. Ruth Lee Jones, 8/29/24, Tuscaloosa, Ala.; d. 12/14/63) is considered one of the most influential, especially to the soul movement of the early sixties. Though her work was often racy and irreverent, she was enormously popular and amassed a number of R&B hits, including the pop number one "Baby (You've Got What It Takes)." Washington, who adored the lavish lifestyle fame brought, would likely have played an even greater role in music had she not died so young (from an overdose of pills taken after too much alcohol). Fortunately, we have her lovely recordings, including the magnificent "What a Difference a Day Makes" to remind us of the gift we once had. (Michael Ochs Archives)

this spread: **Peggy Lee** (b. Norma Jean Egstrom, 5/26/20, Jamestown, N.Dak.) was unsuccessful in her first few attempts to land a good job as a singer, but a meeting with famed band leader Benny Goodman changed all that when he hired her as his replacement singer for Helen Forrest. While in the group, she also met, fell in love, and married their guitarist, Dave Barbour. (The pair formed a professional relationship and composed a number of hits together, including the [rather politically incorrect] smash "Mañana.") Over the course of her career, Lee gained a reputation as a "classy" singer of sophisticated pop tunes and jazz—which she helped introduce to mainstream audiences. Among her many recordings, the sweepingly orchestrated "Lover" (1952) and sensual "Fever" (1958) are music landmarks. No doubt, for someone so beautiful, she would also find her way to Hollywood. But Lee made only a handful of films, including a remake of *Jazz Singer* (1953) and *Pete Kelly's Blues* (1955), for which she received a Supporting Actress Oscar nomination. For all her elegance and charm, it is hard to imagine this: Lee had a terrible childhood. When she was four, Lee's mother died, and for the next eleven years was physically abused by her stepmother; her father, an alcoholic, was taken ill and Lee had to cover for him at his job. But even more amazing, as an adult, Lee never let the hurt show in her work and gave the world a stunning amount of lovely recordings. (Michael Ochs Archives)

inset: Born to a carpenter father and laundress mother, it's a surprise that **Sarah Vaughan** (b. 3/27/24, Newark, N.J.; d. 4/3/90) went into music at all. But in it, she thrived. "The Divine One," as she came to be called, studied piano for ten years and became a church choir organist at age twelve. A talent contest win at—where?!—Harlem's Apollo Theatre brought her to the attention of Billy Eckstine, who asked Vaughan to join his band in 1944. For decades thereafter, she was a dominant force in jazz. By cleverly incorporating more commercial aspects into her recordings, she also became one of the few greats of the genre to experience pop-chart success—the singles "Broken-Hearted Melody" and "Smooth Operator" are sublime and delectable examples. Often cited as one of the greatest singers on record, it would be impossible to name all the artists whom she influenced with her work, but Vaughan herself will never be equalled. (album, *Sarah Vaughan at the Blue Note,* Mercury, 1956)

this spread: If you want to be "bad" just listen to **Eartha Kitt** (b. 1/26/28, North, S.C.), who's made a career out of being naughty (and nice, too!). But who could blame her? Born poor on a cotton plantation, when she was eight years old her mother abandoned her and she was sent to live with an aunt in Harlem. However, this was when she became interested in performing. Accepted by the famed Katherine Dunham dance troupe, Kitt toured Europe, and when the group headed home, she stayed behind in Paris. With singing added to her act, she became a nightclub sensation. (An early admirer, Orson Welles, called her "the most exciting woman in the world" and gave Kitt her acting debut—as "Helen of Troy"—in his 1950 production of *Dr. Faust*.) When she returned stateside, her enthusiastic reception was generally limited—American audiences could not get past her color and enjoy her sexy personality. But New York City ate her up: she was a hit in the Broadway show *New Faces of 1952* with the song "Monotonous." Though she has one of the most recognizable voices on record—"C'est Si Bon," the sendup "I'm Just an Old Fashioned Girl," and the eighties dance hit "Where Is My Man" are a few examples—she begs to be seen in person. And what was once viewed as a hindrance—the blatant sexual mannerisms that "made men nervous"—became precisely what sustained her career for an astounding five decades. (Michael Ochs Archives)

inset: During the fifties, the sexiest white woman "on record" had to be **Julie London** (b. Julie Peck, 9/26/26, Santa Clara, Calif.; d. 10/18/2000). Her sultry, tearful voice made "Cry Me a River" a million-seller, and one of the most romantic pop ballads on record. An inescapably beautiful London also became well known for her album covers, which, rather provocatively, took every opportunity to show off her hourglass figure and ample decolletage. Despite releasing dozens of them over the years, stylish London was never able to duplicate the success of "River" (which can be seen and heard in the 1955 film *The Girl Can't Help It*). Instead she found steadier work in acting—most notably when hired by first husband Jack Webb (of *Dragnet* fame) to appear in the eighties television drama, *Emergency*. (album, *Your Number Please . . .*, Liberty, 1959)

PICTURE POST

MONDAY 26 NOVEMBER 1956

THE COMMUNIST MENACE:
A New Policy needed.
By Edward Hulton

SUEZ frogmen go down
EXCLUSIVE PICTURES

SHIRLEY BASSEY
Girl from Tiger Bay

4D HULTON'S NATIONAL WEEKLY

inset: **Dame Shirley Bassey** (b. 1/8/37, Tiger Bay, Cardiff, Wales) has been dubbed "Bassey the Belter" and "The Tigress of Tiger Bay." Either way, she is easily one of the most exciting, glamourous, and enduring stars ever to have come out of stodgy old England. Perplexingly—despite all the diamonds, furs, and dynamite releases—she has always remained far more popular in the United Kingdom, where her albums have continued to be top sellers for over four decades. Nevertheless, her themes for the James Bond movie series, "Goldfinger" and "Diamonds Are Forever" (and her gay following fave, "This Is My Life"), helped to make Bassey an international celebrity. It may also surprise some familiar with the recent Propellerheads clubland hit, "History Repeating," that this divine diva supplies the sexy vocals. Not bad for a woman who started her career when the Beatles were kids! (magazine, *Picture Post*, England, 11/26/56)

this spread: **Nancy Wilson** (b. 2/20/37, Chillicothe, Ohio) is one of the last great artists to come from the late fifties—the "golden age" of female singers. Signing with Capitol Records in 1960, home to an enormous amount of gifted female (and male) singers, including Frank Sinatra, Nat King Cole, Peggy Lee, and the Beatles, she became the label's second best-selling act—just after the famed moptops! Surprisingly, after recording over sixty albums she has never had a major chart hit, though she won a Best R&B Grammy for her sterling single "How Glad I Am." (portrait of Wilson, c. 1965. Photofest)

this spread: **Natalie Cole** (b. 2/6/50, Los Angeles) has achieved nearly the same amount of fame and accolades as her esteemed father—the legendary Nat King Cole—though the road to success (as it was for her dad) was hardly a smooth one. Early praise was fast and quick. a Grammy for Best New Artist (1975) and major hits like the rousing "This Will Be" and "Our Love." But a growing dependency on drugs pushed her career off course in the early eighties. She rebounded with a group of urban contemporary cuts, including "Pink Cadillac," and "Jump Start." However, it would be her 1991 landmark release of the album *Unforgettable . . . with Love* featuring a technologically enhanced duet with her own father on the title track that would propel her into the front ranks of female vocalists— and earn her an unprecedented seven Grammy awards, including one for Album of the Year. (candid of Cole in performance, c. 1975. David Redfern/Retna)

inset: **Anita Baker** (b. 12/20/57, Toledo, Ohio) had been struggling for years before recognition came her way in the late eighties. With the release of the mega-smash album *Rapture*, it seemed for a moment or two as though no other female song stylist had ever existed. She certainly caught disk jockeys off guard. Normally used to spinning pop, they found themselves adding the soul smashes "Sweet Love" and "Giving You the Best That I've Got" to their playlists. Though her output has decreased measurably in the last decade, Baker remains one of the best female vocalists of the last twenty years—and has an astounding eight Grammy awards to prove it. (CD, *Rapture*, Elektra, 1986)

inset: England has supplied us with a lot of wonderful singers. A favorite is **Lisa Stansfield,** (b. 4/11/66, Rochdale, England) who, like other white soul singers, was first thought to be a black performer. This was compounded by the fact that "All around the World," her international hit, did better on many of the R&B charts than on other ones, as did her follow-ups "You Can't Deny It" and "All Woman." (Music is almost always color-blind, unlike people.) Stansfield's sophisticated music also played well to the late-eighties/early-nineties reemergence of café-esque society. Even though, in many instances, her work was classified as dance music, listeners were just as inclined to sit down and tap along as they were to jump up and boogie. (portrait of Stansfield, c. 1996. Trevor Leighton/Retna)

this spread: **Sade** (b. Helen Folasade Adu, 1/16/59, Ibadan, Nigeria) was something of a music sensation when she hit the charts in the early eighties; it had been years since a female singer caused this much excitement. Her sultry voice and stunning, exotic beauty were instantly captivating to anyone with a good set of ears and eyes. Originally studying to be a fashion designer and modeling part-time, Sade joined a funk music group in London in the early eighties and began to quietly infiltrate the airwaves with her distinctive sound. Her 1985 album *Diamond Life* is one of the top-selling debuts of the eighties and contains the breakout hit, "Smooth Operator," which she co-wrote. By the early nineties her popularity in England waned—though it remained quite high in America—and she discontinued recording. Fortunately, she returned to record stores in late 2000 with the launch of *Lovers Rock.* Sade is a 1985 Grammy winner for Best New Artist. (portrait of Sade, c. 1985. Govert de Roos/Sunshine/Retna)

this spread: As a young teen, **Josephine Baker** (b. Freda McDonald, 6/3/06, St. Louis, Mo.; d. 4/12/75) worked as a housecleaner and babysitter for wealthy white families, who always reminded her "not to kiss the baby." But Baker kept a sense of humor—her act always had a touch of comedy to it— and gained fame (and notoriety) when she moved to France in the twenties and was swept up in the Gaellic fascination with African culture. In Paris's *La Revue Negre*, Baker performed her famous *Danse Sauvage* and became the toast of the town. Equally well known as a dancer and singer, she donned lavish (at times outlandish) costumes that often garnered the most attention. (Her wardrobe, of course, included the legendary banana skirt, which she wore *sans* top.) Despite being one of the wealthiest women in Europe during the twenties, and the most photographed, visits to America were met with disappointment. It seemed audiences were unwilling to accept a sophisticated, talented black woman. (Even the respected *New York Times* called her a "Negro wench," and the famed Stork Club refused to serve her.) Nevertheless, throughout her career, Baker filled European nightclubs and cabarets and worked well into her fifties. A most colorful woman in life, during the Second World War she nobly served for the French Resistance and, upon retirement, supported a group of orphans whom she called, rather appropriately, her "rainbow tribe." You can see and hear Baker in the films *Zou-Zou* and *Princess Tam-Tam*. (FYI: Americans finally overcame their racial indifference to Baker and gave her a glowing reception for her 1973 appearance at Carnegie Hall in New York.) (candid of Baker onstage in Los Angeles, 1951. Archive)

inset: As the first black woman named Miss America, **Vanessa Williams** (b. 3/18/63, Millwood, N.Y.) suffered terribly when she was stripped of the title in 1984. But Williams was able to put the ordeal behind her and rise higher than anyone expected. However, she initially met with great resistance: her first album, *The Right Stuff* (1988), barely got produced because songwriters were reluctant to let her record their songs—it was hard to shake the stigma of a *Penthouse* scandal—but she stuck it out. The album and the single, "Dreamin'" became hits. In 1992, "Save the Best for Last" from *Comfort Zone* was a million-selling smash, as was the Oscar-winning "Colors of the Wind" (from Disney's *Pocahontas*) in 1995. She continually records, but is equally at home on stage or in film, where you may find her listed as Vanessa L. Williams (another actress was already registered as Vanessa Williams and requested that she make the change). (candid of Williams dressed as Josephine Baker for an Apollo Theatre tribute to Motown Records in 1985. Walter McBride/Retna)

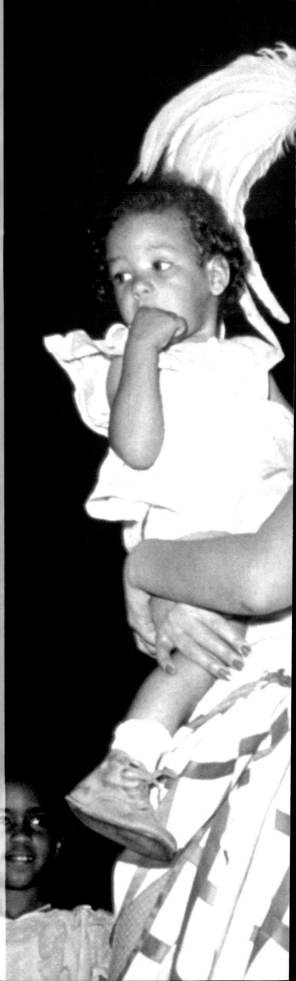

Jane Olivor

Chasing Rain

this spread: **Edith Piaf** (b. Edith Giovanni Gassion, 12/19/15, Paris; d. 10/11/63) was literally born on the streets of Paris—to an acrobat father (whom she adored) and an alcoholic street singer mother (whom she did not). Following in her parents' dubious footsteps, she sang and performed (occasionally acrobatics) for money at many of the city's famed sidewalk cafés. When she was discovered by club owner Louis LePlee and transported out of her life of poverty, she would eventually become one of the world's most highly paid performers. (Tragically, she still died in debt.) LePlee is credited with changing her last name to Piaf, a slang French term for sparrow, thus giving birth to France's beloved "little sparrow." However, LePlee's murder just months after his discovery brought about a temporary halt to the momentum of Piaf's career—many implicated her in the foul deed (though nothing was ever confirmed). As the war years ensued, success continued her way, even though her relationship with occupying German forces caused some concern. What was Piaf's greatest recording? Possibly "La Vie en Rose" (loosely translated into "Life through Rose-Colored Glasses"), written by Piaf herself, or "Non, Je Ne Regrette Rien" ("I Have No Regrets"), her masterpiece of endurance and resilience. Moments of greatest tragedy? When her "secret" lover, Marcel Cerdan, the boxing champion, was killed in an airplane crash on his way to see Piaf; her own daughter's death at age two, from meningitis; or Piaf's lengthy addiction to painkillers that began following a traffic accident. (portrait of Piaf, 1955. Maurice Seymour/MPTV)

inset: Though not nearly as bereft with the same amount of tragedy as Piaf, American chanteuse **Jane Olivor** (b. 1947, New York City) was certainly no stranger to misfortune: her career was sidelined by the untimely death of her husband in 1983. At one time widely compared to Piaf (and Barbra Streisand), Olivor's singing career came to the fore in the mid-seventies, when an underground movement of singers quietly overtook Big Apple cabarets, coffeehouses, and the few remaining nightclubs. Perhaps the song most indicative of Olivor's style is her lullabylike cover of "Chasing Rainbows." (album, *Chasing Rainbows*, Columbia, 1977)

THE ANDREWS SISTERS in HI-FI

this spread: Many of my generation (lthirty-somethings) may best remember **Helen O'Connell** (b. 5/23/20, Lima Ohio; d. 9/9/93) seated in her lofty perch, as the sprightly statistical commentator (and cohost with Bob Barker) for nine years on the Miss Universe pageant. Even I was shocked when I first learned of her extended resume. Singing for band leader Jimmy Dorsey from 1939 to 1943, O'Connell helped place a number of songs into the lexicon of American popular music, including "Tangerine," "Amapola (Pretty Little Poppy)," and her breakout hit, "Green Eyes." Though not possessed of a particularly strong voice, O'Connell gave a delivery so engagingly feminine—and so indicative of the era—that it was worthy of a listen (or two, or three), especially in those more strident times. (portrait of O'Connell, c. 1945 Photofest)

inset: The singing trio of The **Andrews Sisters** (Patty (Marie), b. 2/26/18; Maxene (Angelyn), b. 1/3/16, d. 10/21/95; Laverne (Sofia), b. 7/6/15, d. 5/8/67; all Minneapolis, Minn.) are among the top-selling recording acts of all time—male or female—and *the* most popular female group of the forties. This is not surprising if you read through their list of hits, including "Dont Sit under the Apple Tree," "Bie Mier Mis Du Schoen," "Rum and Coca-Cola," and "I'll Be with You in Apple Blossom Time." Though many of their songs reflect a period in our history fast disappearing from memory, the impact these recordings had on the country (and on servicemen in particular) cannot be underestimated. Along with other great artists of their generation, the Andrews Sisters created a musical force field around democracy—and when victory came, they gave the people something to sing about. (album, *The Andrews Sisters in Hi-Fi*, Capitol, 1956)

for the boys

inset: The top-selling female performer of the fifties, **Patti Page** (b. Clara Ann Fowler, 11/8/27, Tulsa, Okla.) got her name from a late-forties Tulsa radio show entitled *Meet Patti Page.* (I can't imagine why she felt that her real name wouldn't have worked just as well!) A unique and inventive singer, Page often used different versions of her own voice to create a fuller, choral-like effect on her songs. If you are a big fan of music from the Eisenhower era, Page's playlist is as complete a musical representation of that golden time as one can get. Together, hits like "I Don't Care if the Sun Don't Shine," "Mister and Mississippi," "I Went to Your Wedding," "How Much Is That Doggie in the Window," and "Cross over the Bridge" form a melodic cornucopia reflective of a period at the cultural crossroads. On a simpler note, songs like "Allegheny Moon" and "Old Cape Cod" are timelessly romantic. Her biggest hit (and the biggest single of the entire decade), "Tennessee Waltz," was a thirteen-week chart-topper that is considered the first country-to-pop crossover hit. Page had her own television variety show (from 1955 to 1958) and received a long overdue Grammy in 1998 for her *Live at Carnegie Hall —The Fiftieth Anniversary Concert* (Best Traditional Pop Performance). (album, *Page 4*, Mercury, 1956)

this spread: Next in line as the top-selling female performer of the fifties was **Kay Starr** (b. Katherine LaVerne Starks, 7/21/22, Dougherty, Okla.), who, like so many female singers, started out singing in a big band. Her hit as a solo artist (among many), "Rock and Roll Waltz," was an interesting composition that tried valiantly to bridge together two wildly disparate genres of music. Its enormous success (six weeks at number one) says as much about the innocence of the time as it does for the merits of the song. Her even bigger hit (ten weeks on top) is the gutsy "Wheel of Fortune," with its underlying theme of desperation—set to sound effects and instrumentation that truly conjure up gaming tables. (Michael Ochs Arcives)

CUSTOM HIGH FIDELITY

PAGE 4

PATTI PAGE

A COLLECTION OF HER MOST FAMOUS SONGS

RCA VICTOR
A "New Orthophonic" High Fidelity Recording
LPM-1214

Bouquet of Blues
DINAH SHORE

this spread: So did we all think MTV was the first entertainment to showcase popular music? Not if you read through television history books. Though "pop" charts had existed for some time, once the idea first struck to televise them it would revolutionize both industries. When *Your Hit Parade* made it onto the air in 1950, the world was eager to watch and listen. Each broadcast featured the week's top tunes, as sung by a regular cast of talented singers. **Gisele MacKenzie** (b. Gisele LeFleche, 1/10/27, Winnipeg, Canada) was one of them. MacKenzie garnered lots of praise and attention (including three Emmy nominations as best female musical talent—how's that for a timely category!) for her appearances. However, in 1957, she, along with the entire original ensemble, was replaced by new talent in an effort to appeal to younger audiences. So even *that* troublesome habit isn't new, either! (candid of MacKenzie on the set of *The Gisele MacKenzie Show,* 1957. Sid Avery/MPTV)

inset: Tennessee's singing sweetheart, **Dinah Shore** (b. Frances Rose Shore, 3/1/17, Winchester, Tenn.; d. 2/24/94) first sang with Xavier Cugat's band, then on the radio, and eventually amassed seventy hit songs (including "Buttons and Bows," "I'll Walk Alone," and the charming novelty, "Shoo-Fly Pie and Apple Pan Dowdy," which was revived recently in a Mercedes-Benz commercial). During the war, she was the first female performer to entertain troops on the front lines and was given a medal for her generosity. She also became the first woman to host her own variety show on prime-time television. By the seventies, her appearances had morphed into a role as chat-show hostess, and her longevity in the medium netted an unprecedented eight Emmy and one Peabody awards. She enjoyed a long marriage to western-movie stud George Montgomery, and a May-Septemberish romance with a younger Burt Reynolds during the seventies (the risqué nature of the relationship did little to quell her popularity). Incidentally, the golf tourney she founded in 1972, the Dinah Shore Classic, was one of the very first major moneymaking sports events for women. (album, *Bouquet of Blues*, RCA-Victor, 1956)

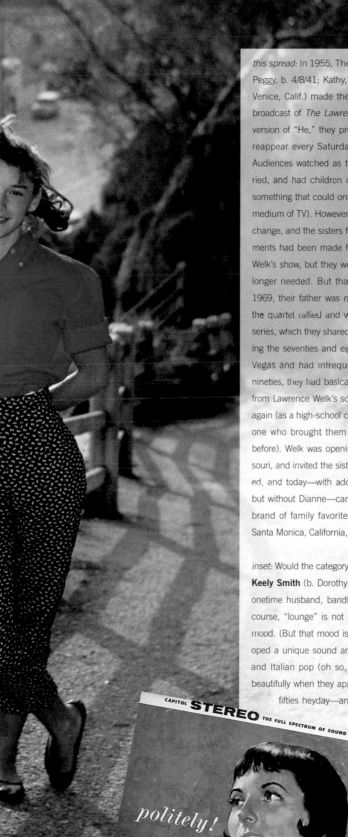

this spread: In 1955, The **Lennon Sisters** (Dianne, b. 12/1/39; Peggy, b. 4/8/41; Kathy, b. 8/2/43; and Janet, b. 6/15/46, all Venice, Calif.) made their television debut on the Christmas broadcast of *The Lawrence Welk Show.* Singing an acapella version of "He," they proved so popular that Welk had them reappear every Saturday night for the next thirteen years. Audiences watched as these four little angels grew up, married, and had children of their own (rather remarkable, and something that could only have been possible with the "new" medium of TV). However, the late sixties was a time of cultural change, and the sisters felt they needed to move on. Arrangements had been made for them to appear less frequently on Welk's show, but they were notified that their talents were no longer needed. But that was the least of their troubles. In 1969, their father was murdered by a crazed fan. Somehow the quartet rallied and went on to have their own short-lived series, which they shared with comedian Jimmy Durante. During the seventies and eighties, they performed mainly in Las Vegas and had infrequent television appearances. By the nineties, they had basically retired from show business. A call from Lawrence Welk's son, Larry Jr., got them started all over again (as a high-school classmate of Dianne's, he was also the one who brought them to his father's attention forty years before). Welk was opening a music theater in Branson, Missouri, and invited the sisters to become regulars. They accepted, and today—with additional family members at their side but without Dianne—can still be seen performing their sweet brand of family favorites. (candid of the Lennon sisters in Santa Monica, California, 1958. Corbis)

inset: Would the category of "lounge" music even exist without **Keely Smith** (b. Dorothy Smith, 3/9/32, Norfolk, Va.) and her onetime husband, bandleader Louis Prima? Possibly not. Of course, "lounge" is not really a genre of music, more like a mood. (But that mood is always a good one.) The two developed a unique sound and act: a mixture of jazz, light blues, and Italian pop (oh so, cosmopolitan!) that came together beautifully when they appeared in Las Vegas—during its late-fifties heyday—and on their swinging cover of Johnny Mercer and Harold Arlen's "That Old Black Magic." Smith's voice paired just as well with ballads, too (but the same could not be said for her marriage with Prima; she divorced him in 1961, citing extreme mental cruelty). (album; *Politely,* Capitol, 1958)

CAPITOL **STEREO** THE FULL SPECTRUM OF SOUND

politely!

KEELY SMITH

with Billy May and his orchestra

this spread: Originally, a young **Doris Day** (b. Doris Von Kappelhoff, 4/3/22, Cincinnati, Ohio) dreamed of being a ballerina, but a car accident ended her early aspirations. However, the dance world's loss was the music world's gain. Her early years as a band singer were responsible for at least one massive hit, "Sentimental Journey." When she entered into film (in 1948's *Romance on the High Seas*, featuring the Oscar-nominated classic "It's Magic") it was like a tidal wave. Each subsequent appearance only intensified the public's attraction. By the sixties, she was film's most popular female star. Day introduced several songs into the annals of all-time favorite pop standards, such as "Secret Love" and "Whatever Will Be, Will Be (Qué Sera, Sera)"—both of which were also Oscar winners. Married three times, Day discovered only after the death of her last husband, Marty Melcher, in 1968, that a mismanaged and squandered fortune (at the hands of Melcher) would necessitate her move into television. Fortunately, *The Doris Day Show* (1968–1973) proved an easy hit among fans—and her financial woes subsided. Winner of three Golden Globe awards—because they had a comedy category!—but no Oscar, and a well-known pet lover and activist, Day is now an innkeeper currently living in Carmel, California. (portrait of Day, c. 1956. Wallace Seawell/MPTV)

inset: **Rosemary Clooney** (b. 5/23/28, Maysville, Ky.) also began as a band singer, but would not enjoy the same level of success of her contemporaries until she went solo in 1949. Clooney's first major hit was the provocative "Come on-a My House" (1951), and her biggest release was "Hey There" (1956) from the Broadway score of *Pajama Game* (the 1957 film version of which, ironically, starred Doris Day). Her tumultuous marriage to acclaimed actor Jose Ferrer gave her five children *and* a much-chronicled nervous breakdown—that sidelined her career until it was resurrected in 1976. Clooney is also the aunt of actor George Clooney. (album, *Swing around Rosie*, Coral, 1958)

you oughta be in pictures

ORIGINAL SOUND TRACK ALBUM OF THE MUSICAL MOTION PICTURE OF THE '70'S

Universal presents

Sweet Charity

Shirley MacLaine ★ Sammy Davis, Jr.

MCA

inset: **Shirley MacLaine** (b. Shirley MacLean Beatty, 4/24/34, Richmond, Va.) owes the start of her career to the original stage version of *Pajama Game*. As understudy, she once took over the lead when illness struck star Carol Haney—and as they say, a star was born. (Incidentally, Haney was a very gifted performer, whom few remember today. In a strange twist, she did have a part in the 1957 film version of *Pajama Game*.) MacLaine almost immediately went on to movie stardom; her first feature was *The Trouble with Harry* (1955) for Alfred Hitchcock (how's that for a start?). Despite the background in song-and-dance, MacLaine appeared in only two movie musicals, *Can-Can* (1960) and *Sweet Charity* (directed by Bob Fosse in 1969). When she entered film, musicals were already on their way out and this accounted for their notable absence on her resume. However, she made up for this with a number of acclaimed television variety specials—one of which gave her an Emmy. A six-time Oscar nominee and a one-time winner, for *Terms of Endearment* (1984), MacLaine is also the recipient of six Golden Globes. (soundtrack album, *Sweet Charity*, MCA, 1969)

this spread: **Gwen Verdon** (b. 1/13/25, Los Angeles; d. 10/18/2000) is often linked with her husband, Bob Fosse, but there is little doubt this tomboy who loved being "one of the boys" would have placed among theater's greats by virtue of her striking talent alone. Verdon enjoyed a long string of successes on the Great White Way, including *Damn Yankees* (1955)—in a role she re-created on film, where you can watch her famous rendition of "Whatever Lola Wants." This film was produced by the same team responsible for *Pajama Game*, *New Girl in Town*, and *Redhead* (Fosse's directorial debut). She also had her big breakthrough in—and first Tony, among four, for (if you haven't already guessed)—*Can-Can*. Her last major theater triumph was as the lead in—what else?—*Sweet Charity* (under the direction of hubby Fosse, and based on the 1957 Fellini film *Nights of Cabiria*). Married to Fosse in 1960, she never officially divorced him, even after their separation in the mid-seveties. (publicity still of Verdon for the 1957 film version of *Damn Yankees*. Photofest)

When **Liza Minnelli** (b. 3/12/46, Los Angeles) and her mother **Judy Garland** (b. Frances Gumm, 6/10/22, Grand Rapids, Minn.; d. 6/22/69) both appeared onstage at the Palladium in London, it was clear to mom that her daughter was on the threshold of stardom. Their subsequent appearance together on Judy's television show in 1963 only reinforced her feelings—and that of the enrapt audience. Unquestionably, a star had been born to a born star—and the magic would continue for generations to come.

Though possibly too much has been made of the personal, professional, and physical turmoils of the lives of Garland and Minnelli, their combined contribution to film, stage, and recordings far outshines the murky shadows cast by tabloids and critics. Some notable highlights: four Oscar nominations, and one win, for Minnelli in *Cabaret* (1972); a special 1939 Academy Award to Garland for her work in *The Wizard of Oz*; an Emmy for Liza's TV special, *Liza with a Z*; two Emmy nominations for Garland; six Golden Globe nominations, and two wins for Liza; two Golden Globe awards to Garland—one honorary, the other for *A Star is Born* (1954); two Tonys for Minnelli (*Flora, the Red Menace* [1964] and *The Act* [1977]); a Grammy Legend award to Minnelli; a Lifetime Achievement Grammy and Album of the Year award for Garland for *Judy at Carnegie Hall* (1961); and possibly most noteworthy of all, the recent listing of Garland's "Somewhere over the Rainbow" as the most popular recording of the twentieth century by the RIAA. (Incidentally, Minnelli can share some of the credit of her success with Bob Fosse too, who choreographed and directed her in *Cabaret*. The role of Sally Bowles also included a Kander/Ebb song written especially for Minnelli, "Maybe This Time.") (candid of Minnelli and Garland performing on *The Judy Garland Show*, 1963. Everett)

Bernadette Peters

Vargas

this spread: "There's no business like show business," and no one understood its ups and downs better than the indomitable **Ethel Merman** (b. Ethel Agnes Zimmermann, 1/16/08, Queens, N.Y.; d. 2/15/84). Although this Broadway belter was not a stranger to film, she was frequently bypassed for movie roles (for parts she successfully originated onstage) in favor of stars considered more marketable—Betty Hutton, Lucille Ball, Ann Sothern, Rosalind Russell, to name a few. This came as no surprise to many accomplished Broadway performers, but it was no less disappointing for the individual or fan—to say nothing of the often disappointing results. Nevertheless, Merman became the quintessential Broadway musical comedy star. Untrained as a singer, her booming voice and brash personality were perfect for the stage; simply, no one could deliver the goods like Merman. Of the many, many musicals she made, the most memorable are *Anything Goes, Annie Get Your Gun, Gypsy* (including her classic rendition of "Everything's Coming up Roses"), and *Call Me Madam* (which, ironically, was the only role that won her a Tony—and one that she marvelously re-created onscreen in 1953—for which she received a Golden Globe, too!) (publicity still of Merman in the film version of *Call Me Madam.* Archive)

inset: Not surprisingly, even awards for roles Merman originated on stage invariably went to performers in subsequent versions. Revivals of *Gypsy* won Tonys for Angela Lansbury and Tyne Daly, and another went to **Bernadette Peters** (b. Bernadette Lazzara, 2/28/44, Queens, N.Y.) in the recent restaging of *Annie Get Your Gun.* This was the second Tony for Peters, who is one of the few current theatre performers evocative of earlier talent. The first was for *Song and Dance* (1985). A gifted comedian as well, her most memorable film role was in the unusual musical *Pennies from Heaven* (1981). Under the direction of Herbert Ross, Peters was featured in a number of lavish production numbers. She succeeded valiantly—winning a Golden Globe—but the somber tone of the movie did not attract an audience. Peters also had a recording career, which yielded her the top-40 hit "Gee Whiz" in 1979. (album, *Bernadette Peters*, MCA, 1980)

inset: **Betty Hutton** (b. Elizabeth June Thornburg, 2/26/21, Battle Creek, Mich.) was a top musical film star for Paramount Studios in the forties, combining a melancholy voice (the 1947 Oscar-nominated ballad "I Wish I Didn't Love You So" from *The Perils of Pauline* is an exceptionally lovely example) with an acute flair for comedy (*The Miracle of Morgan's Creek*, 1944). However, Hutton's popularity dissipated in the fifties—due in no small part to her own difficult temperament—and she went from being one of the richest women in Hollywood to relative obscurity and poverty by the sixties. Incidentally, Hutton scored a success with the musical *Annie Get Your Gun*, but she was not the first to be chosen to play in the film version. That distinction went to Judy Garland. However, in one of the worst moments of her career, Garland was fired because of professional differences. (sheet music, "I Wish I Didn't Love You So," Susan Publications, 1947)

this spread: **Mary Martin** (b. 12/1/13, Weatherford, Tex.; d. 12/3/90) is one of Broadway's legendary stars, but the fact that her success did not carry over into film is considered one of entertainment's great mysteries. However, the talent that Tinseltown could never quite tap had none of the same problem onstage. Martin was the original Maria in *The Sound of Music* and Nellie Fornbush in *South Pacific* (though she lost both movie roles). She soared high as Peter Pan at the Winter Garden Theatre and in a historic televised broadcast (watched by nearly half the country's population in 1955!). All three roles won her Tonys for Best Actress in a musical, and the TV version of *Pan* won her an Emmy. Arguably, of the many songs she introduced to the public, her most memorable may be Cole Porter's "My Heart Belongs to Daddy," from the 1938 musical *Leave It to Me*. (By the way, though Martin and Ethel Merman were contemporaries, their two styles were so dissimilar that their work rarely overlapped. However, there were exceptions, as you can see in this photo: a candid of Martin on the set of the 1958 television version of *Annie Get Your Gun*. Some parts sure do get around! Gerald Smith/MPTV)

I WISH I DIDN'T LOVE YOU SO

BY FRANK LOESSER

SPECIAL PICTURE RELEASE

THE PERILS OF PAULINE

SCORE
Rumble, Rumble, Rumble
I Wish I Didn't Love You So
The Sewing Machine
Poppa Don't Preach To Me

Paramount Presents
The PERILS OF PAULINE
IN TECHNICOLOR
BETTY HUTTON
and
JOHN LUND

Susan Publications, INC

FAMOUS MUSIC CORPORATION
1619 Broadway, N. Y. C. Sole Selling Agents

inset: Martin lost the film role of Nellie Fornbush, from the Pulitzer Prize-winning musical *South Pacific*, to pretty and perky **Mitzi Gaynor** (b. Franceska Mitzi Gerber, 9/4/30, Chicago). However, Gaynor was not first choice; that honor went to Doris Day, for whom it would have likely been a perfect part. But Day left before filming began, after she and the director, Joshua Logan, had a mild dispute. The finished version of *South Pacific* is an interesting example of how often the best of intentions can go awry. Despite the fact that it was beautifully produced and a very successful release—and Gaynor is far from inadequate in the lead role—the work has been widely panned for not capturing the intensity and essence of the stage original. (However, I recommend you view it and judge for yourself; Gaynor was perfect singing "Cockeyed Optimist.") (soundtrack album, *South Pacific*, RCA, 1958)

this spread: Delightful **Shirley Jones** (b. 3/31/34, Smithton, Pa.) did not originate the character of Laurey in the stage version of *Oklahoma!* (for heaven's sake, she would have been less than ten years old!); that honor goes to Joan Roberts. But Jones did play the part on Broadway (prior to its closing) before inheriting the coveted film role. Unfortunately, Jones, like Shirley MacLaine, started in film musicals when the category was fast losing ground and appeared in only a handful: *Oklahoma!* (1955), *Carousel* (1956), *April Love* (1957), and *Music Man* (1962), which though a little high in the corn count features Jone's voice at its best. This 1960 Oscar winner for *Elmer Gantry* (yes, she went against type and played a prostitute!) was the only member of the cast of the television show *The Partridge Family* to do his or her own singing—except for her stepson David. (film still of Jones from the musical *Oklahoma!*, 1955. Everett)

Fresh from a success on television with their original work, *Cinderella* (cast with ingenue Julie Andrews), the team of Rodgers and Hammerstein—who wrote the scores of *South Pacific* and *Oklahoma!*—were eager to dispell any lingering doubts left by the less-than-stellar success of their most recent theater piece, *Pipe Dreams*. The stage musical *Flower Drum Song* did the trick. (However, by today's standards it is considered more a charming novelty than a substantial addition to musical theater.) *Flower*—which introduced "Love, Look Away" and "Grant Avenue"—tells the story of a Chinese man (at the time played by Anglo actor Larry Blyden) who is promised to marry one woman, played by **Miyoshi Umeki** (b. 4/3/29, Otaru, Japan), while seemingly in love with another, portrayed by **Pat Suzuki** (b. Chiyoko Suzuki, 9/23/34, Cressey, Calif.). The romantic triangle story was far from new, but its juxtaposition with generational differences in an Asian family was. Set in San Francisco (where else?), *Flower* was directed by Gene Kelly and choreographed by Carol Haney (see page 70).

At the time, both female leads were riding high on a wave of popularity for all things Eastern. Suzuki—who was "discovered" by Bing Crosby—was in the midsts of a highly successful recording and nightclub career (her repertoire included a powerhouse rendition of "I Enjoy Being a Girl," from the score of *Flower*). Umeki—who was "discovered" by Arthur Godfrey on his *Talent Scouts* show—had just entered film and scored an amazing success *and* Oscar win (as Best Supporting Actress) with her debut in *Sayonara* (1957). (Incidentally, Umeki re-created her *Flower* role onscreen; Suzuki did not.) The twosome also had the landmark distinction of appearing on the cover of *Time* magazine. When Asian-infused entertainment crested in the early sixties, Suzuki went on to marry noted photographer Mark Shaw (Kennedy family portraiture), to sing with Frank Sinatra at JFK's 1961 inaugural ball, and play a role in the seventies sitcom, *Mr T. and Tina* (the first featuring an Asian-American family). Umeki appeared in a few more films and had a recurring role in television's *The Courtship of Eddie's Father*. (*inset*: album, *Miyoshi*, Mercury, 1957; *this spread*: candid of Suzuki in performance of the Broadway show *Flower Drum Song*, 1958. Photofest)

this spread: **Dame Julie Andrews** (b. Julia Elizabeth Wells, 10/1/35, Walton-on-Thames, England), that most beloved of all stage and screen stars, began her career when it was discovered by her parents that their little girl possessed an unusual, and quite lovely, four-octave singing voice. She performed through her childhood and teen years, before landing on Broadway in 1954 with her first hit, *The Boyfriend.* Of course, the part she became famous for was as Eliza Doolittle, in *My Fair Lady* (1956). As every seasoned theater buff knows, she was not asked to reprise her role in the lavish screen version—that went to loverly, non-singing Audrey Hepburn. But she continued her *reign* as Queen Guinevere in 1960's *Camelot*, and as Cinderella for television. By 1964 (the year of the film version of *My Fair Lady*), Andrews scored a major triumph by appearing in the delightful Disney feature *Mary Poppins*—and won herself an Oscar. Her stupendous hit *Sound of Music* (in the role originated by Mary Martin) the following year would be the second of six successful movie musicals. The last was 1980's *Victor/Victoria*. The stage version of *Victor/Victoria* in 1995 was her most recent success on Broadway, but a throat injury is expected to keep her splendid voice away from the ears of anxious fans for quite some time—if not indefinitely. Andrews is an Emmy, multi-Golden Globe, and Grammy award winner (for the score from *Mary Poppins*), but, surprisingly, *not* the recipient of a Tony! (candid of Andrews at the 1966 Academy Awards ceremony. Archive)

inset: Before originating the Broadway role of Maria in the musical *West Side Story*, **Carol Lawrence** (b. Carol Laraia, 9/5/34, Melrose Park, Il.) was a featured performer, along with Eartha Kitt, in the curious stage vehicle *New Faces of 1952* (the show also introduced comedians Paul Lynde, Alice Ghostley, and Mel Brooks). Even after her success in *Story*, the film role was given to Natalie Wood. But she rebounded nicely by appearing in dozens of television shows and more musicals. She married singing heartthrob Robert Goulet in 1963 (though they divorced in 1980). (FYI: Lawrence and Julie Andrews share this interesting connection: it was obvious even before they were hired that neither Natalie Wood nor Audrey Hepburn could adequately sing, so their voices were dubbed (quelle insult!) by noted behind-the-scenes talent Marni Nixon, who also "sang" for Deborah Kerr in 1956's *The King and I.* Kerr snatched the role from Gertrude Lawrence. Nixon does appear onscreen as Sister Sophia in *The Sound of Music.*) (cast album, *West Side Story*, Columbia, 1957)

this spread: Does **Carol Channing** (b. 1/31/21, Seattle, Wash.) believe "diamonds are a girl's best friend"? Well she should, considering she introduced the line back in 1949, with the musical Gentlemen Prefer Blondes. However, Channing may feel that a girl's best friend is a gifted composer, one who can create a singing part that will keep her in jewels and furs— which she can then buy for herself! In Channing's case, that person would be Jerry Herman, whom she has to thank for the role of Dolly Levi—which she has performed a thousand-plus times (including once for the first public appearance of Jacqueline Kennedy and her children after the president's death). The part is also the only one to earn Channing a Tony. She won the statuette in competition with Barbra Streisand (for Funny Girl), the actress who took the film role. There we go again! Channing also had just won a 1967 Golden Globe for Thoroughly Modern Millie. (candid of Channing performing in Hello, Dolly, 1964. TimePix)

inset: Though the vast majority know her as Jessica Fletcher from the long-running series, Murder, She Wrote, **Angela Lansbury** (b. 10/16/25, London) has a list of stellar credits as long as this book. She debuted in the film classic Gaslight (1944) and received her first Oscar nomination. We then heard her warble "Little Yellow Bird" in yet another classic, The Picture of Dorian Gray (1945). It became her second nominated role—a third was for a nasty turn in The Manchurian Candidate (1962). Her success carried over to Broadway in the sixties, beginning with a lead role in A Taste of Honey, then a first Tony win for Jerry Herman's smash, Mame (which she also revived years later). She won a second Tony for Dear World, a third for playing the lead in a revival of Gypsy, and a fourth as the pie-baking wife in Stephen Sondheim's bloody good Sweeney Todd. (candid of Lansbury performing in Mame, 1966. TimePix)

inset: **Fanny Brice** (b. Fanny Borach, 10/29/1891, New York City; d. 5/29/51) made a career out of getting audiences to laugh with characters like Baby Snooks (a smash on radio), but she was at her most endearing when she sang. Dressed in the rags of a street waif, Brice made those same audiences cry with her tearful rendition of "My Man." (Give it a close listen, even though the original lyrics are shamefully dated today.) Composer/lyricist Jule Styne paid Brice the ultimate tribute years later by writing the musical *Funny Girl.* (magazine, *Stage After Dark*, 7/38)

this spread: **Barbra Streisand** (b. 4/24/42, Brooklyn, N.Y.) is "by far the greatest star" (at least to her millions of devoted admirers). But "people who need people" are often surprised to learn that their "secondhand rose" has a notorious resistance to fan worship. But "don't rain on her parade," because she always comes through with some "main event" that will please critics and audiences alike. Besides, it would have been near impossible for her to remain immune, "ageless, and evergreen" to the constant onslaught of attention. We expect all our celebrities to behave admirably at all times. But "for Pete's sake," guys, "how lucky can you get?" You have nearly four decades of work to help remember "the way we were" and still have that beautiful "one voice" to carry us "somewhere" into the future. (I know, you're thinking this could go on "all night long." Well, "nuts" to that!) (FYI: the song "My Man" was left out of the stage version of *Funny Girl*—but was gloriously reinstated in the 1968 film, resulting in one of the best musical finales on celluloid.) (film still of Streisand from *Funny Lady*, 1975. Mel Traxel/MPTV)

i know a place

PETULA CLARK COLOR MY WORLD
WHO AM I

this spread: Songwriters Burt Bacharach and Hal David couldn't have asked for more when they met up with **Dionne Warwick** (b. 12/12/41, East Orang, N.J.) in 1963. Without missing a beat, she was able to work her voice through their often complex arrangements in a way no other singer was (or is) able to do. From their first hit, the soul-tinged "Don't Make Me Over" through to the defiant "Walk on By" and "I'll Never Fall in Love Again," the poignant "Do You Know the Way to San Jose" (Warwick got a key to the city, too!), and their last Scepter hit recording, the melancholy "Make it Easy on Yourself," the trio lent a soft, sophisticated edge to the turbulent soundtrack of the sixties. Amazingly, most of Warwick's highest charters occurred apart from her longtime collaborators. The splendid "(Theme from) The Valley of the Dolls," a number-two hit, was composed by Andre Previn. "Then Came You" (with the Spinners) was number one in 1974. "I'll Never Love This Way Again" went to five, thanks to Barry Manilow. "Heartbreaker" by the brothers Gibb broke into the top 10. And, her quartet outing "That's What Friends Are For" (with Stevie Wonder, Elton John, and Gladys Knight) was her biggest single to date. Warwick—whose cousin is, yes, the divine Whitney Houston—remains a popular favorite *despite* forays into questionable undertakings. But it doesn't take a psychic to understand why: her recordings appeal to the heart—where's the bad luck in that? (candid of Warwick in performance, 1965. David Redfern/Retna)

inset: **Petula Clark** (b. 11/15/32, Ewell, England) had already made dozens of films in England and worked in France (where she is considered a French singer) before her hits "Downtown" and "I Know a Place" (both Grammy winners for Best Rock and Roll performance) established her as a star on American soil. For such a pretty singer could movie stardom be too lofty a dream? Unfortunately, yes. She entered into films specifically to resuscitate musicals, but far too late to make an impact. (But still try to tune into *Finian's Rainbow* [1968] just to hear her splendid renditions of the classics "Look to the Rainbow" and "How Are Things in Glocca Morra.") She has, however, found a welcome home on the stage and is credited with playing the role of Norma Desmond in *Sunset Boulevard* longer than any other actress. (album, *Color My World*)

this spread: At its peak, it has been suggested that **Karen Carpenter** (b. 3/2/50, New Haven, Conn.; d. 2/5/83) had a voice that could rival Barbra Streisand's. I don't know how accurate this statement is, but I do know in terms of sheer emotional force, Carpenter was a close second, if not an equal to the balladeer. Unfortunately, Carpenter died so young—and at a career low—for us to properly weigh the odds. When she and brother Richard first hit the charts in 1970, they were a welcome diversion from the anarchistic style of post-sixties rock and roll. "Close to You," their initial release, was a number-one single and was quickly followed by a succession of alternatingly plaintive and optimistically up-tempo ditties. However, their sweet brand of music was far too saccharine for some, and the duo stopped having hits by the late seventies. Today, Carpenter is remembered as a high-profile victim of the then little-known disorder of *anorexia nervosa*—which is characterized by feelings of deep self-loathing and depression. A tragedy all the more poignant when you measure the "love" she gave the world with her music. (candid of Carpenter in performance, c. 1972. Everett)

inset: Born the daughter of an Austrian baroness and a university lecturer, you would think an easy life was set for pretty **Marianne Faithfull** (b. 12/19/46, London) and in the beginning it was. At a party, she met Rolling Stones manager, Andrew Oldham, who was so impressed that he signed her immediately. Ironically, her association with partying and the Stones—especially Mick Jagger—would spell her downfall. A number of times, Faithfull had to cancel entire tours because of drug-related illness or injury. A suicide attempt, after her breakup with Jagger, caused her to withdraw completely from the public. But ultimately, she became a survivor, not a statistic, of the wanton excesses of the sixties. In 1979, she released her seminal album *Broken English*. With her once-innocent voice now replaced by a harsher rasp, and songs informed by years of experience, she was more expressive and personal than ever before. It became her most-acclaimed musical endeavor. (Michael Ochs Archives)

showstopper

this spread: Arguably, no other performer embodies the qualities of "showstopper" better than that most divine of God's creations: **Cher** (b. Cherilyn Sarkisian LaPierre, 5/20/46, El Centro, Calif.). From the first moment we laid eyes on her almost-too-perfect figure and heard her velvety smooth voice—could it actually be over thirty years now?—we were hooked. Like her contemporaries—Olivia Newton-John and Diana Ross—Cher's solo career was built on single-driven rather than album-driven success. Nevertheless, her early seventies hits "Gypsys, Tramps, and Thieves" and "Half-Breed" were perfectly suited to the public persona of the "dark lady" of music. But can anything compare to the dozens of gleeful moments when the world tuned in weekly to *The Sonny and Cher Comedy Hour* (1971–1977) and *Cher* (1975–1976) to see what new Bob Mackie-sequined confection barely (and I mean barely!) covered her willowy frame, and then listen to her cover of that moment's hottest pop tune? Possibly not, my friend. The undisputed fact that she has remained so long at the top of a business known for its quick disappearances is testament to her unique attraction. From an Oscar (for 1987's *Moonstruck*) to, finally, a Grammy in 1999 (for Best Dance Song—*Believe*), she has come a very, very long way, baby! and taken all of us along for a dazzling and exciting ride. (candid of Cher in performance on the *Sonny and Cher Show*, 1973. Gabi Rona/MPTV)

inset: While Donny (and brothers Osmond) became stars—thanks to hordes of screaming girls—baby sister **Marie Osmond** (b. 10/13/59, Ogden, Utah) quietly waited for her turn. But instead of vying for attention in the same sugary realm as her siblings, little Marie wisely opted to go south. The result was "Paper Roses," which made her (then) the youngest singer to hit the top of the country chart. This immediate success led TV execs to ponder the idea of pairing pretty Marie with equally so Donny on prime time. The notion took, and when it did the world was never quite the same. For four years the nation fell under the spell of their teenaged Princess Charming, who loved to poke fun at the hapless Prince (à la Cher and Sonny). The two also collected a handful of hits, including "I'm Leaving It All up to You" and "Morning Side of the Mountain," but fans will likely remember the duo singing these immortal lines: "She's a little bit country, and he's a little bit rock 'n' roll!" (candid of Osmond in performance on *The Donny and Marie Show*, c. 1978. Michael Ochs Archives)

Someday Sweetheart

Sophie Tucker's *Sensational Hit!*

by *Spikes & Spikes*

inset: The "last of the red hot mamas" was **Sophie Tucker** (b. Sophie Kalish, 1/13/1884; d. 2/9/66). A major vaudeville star who was part of the Ziegfeld Follies, Tucker turned to movies, television, and more recordings when the popularity of the circuit went on the wane. As singer and actress, she relied heavily on humor to attract audiences, but more importantly, Tucker took being overdressed, overripe, and overweight and made it work to her advantage. Though a great deal of her work has never been heard (or seen) by present-day audiences—including her most famous song "Some of These Days"—covert sexual and adult content, combined with a self-effacing personality, makes Tucker cannily relevant to today's audiences. (sheet music, "Someday Sweetheart," Melrose Bros. Publishing)

this spread: The story of **Bette Midler** (b. 12/1/45, Honolulu, Hawaii) including her rise to fame from within the gay underworld—the Continental Baths, to be exact, with Barry Manilow at her side—has long since been entered into the history books of pop culture. Her uncanny sense of comedic timing and a charmingly vulgar wit is also now part of the same lore (and Midler is the first to admit that her early bodacious manner owed a great deal to "Soph" Tucker). However, what many are fast forgetting is the musical contribution this divine woman made. I'm not speaking of her huge hits "The Rose," "Wind beneath My Wings" (Grammy winner for Record and Song of the Year, 1990), and "From a Distance," which are all marvelous. But does anyone remember how Midler brought back forties "boogie-woogie"—at least for a few brief moments—in the early seventies? One of Midler's first big chart successes (after "Do Ya Wanna Dance") was the 1973 cover of the Andrews Sisters' classic "Boogie Woogie Bugle Boy" (which she happened to take higher on the charts than they did!). That year she also took home the Grammy for Best New Artist. (candid of Midler in performance with the Harlettes, at the Greek Forum, Los Angeles, 1979. Nancy Barr/Retna)

Another act that rose to fame on a wave of forties nostalgia were the **Pointer Sisters** (*left to right:* June, b. 11/30/53; Anita, b. 1/23/48, Bonnie, b. 8/11/51; and Ruth, b. 3/19/46; all Oakland, Calif.). Despite both parents being ministers, the sisters went the secular music route and sang backup for such varied artists as Boz Scaggs and Grace Slick. In 1973 they released their first family effort, *The Pointer Sisters*, which showcased the be-bop harmonies that captivated listeners. (They even styled themselves in fashions of the era—platform shoes, floral-print dresses, hairdos in snoods, and the added pizazz of feather boas.) However, their music selections were quite varied: the early hit "Yes We Can, Can" was an infectious ditty with a hint of soul; "How Long (I Betcha Got a Chick on the Side)" was their first to go number-one R&B; and "Fairytale" was a 1974 Grammy winner in the country category (based on the single's success, the sisters became the first black females to appear at Nashville's Grand Ole Opry). The act broke up in 1977, but regrouped for an astounding "comeback" in 1979—without sister Bonnie (who once humorously called the group "the hottest thing to come outta Oakland since the Black Panthers!"). She embarked on a solo career with the release of the heavenly dance classic, "Heaven Must Have Sent You." The new threesome shed their former feathers in exchange for a more modern approach to music. The result was a string of remarkable successes: a smoldering cover of Bruce Springsteen's "Fire"; "He's So Shy"; "Slow Hand"; the electronically enhanced "Jump" and "Automatic" (both Grammy-winning examples of their amazing vocal skillls); and "I'm So Excited." (Michael Ochs Archives)

Sometimes all it takes is one song to make an act immortal. Certainly, bestowing such an honor can be debated for the group **Sister Sledge** (*left to right:* Debra, b. 1955; Kathy, b. 1959; Kim, b. 1958; Joni, b. 1957; all Philadelphia). Despite years of minor success on the R&B charts, it wasn't until a fortuitous linkup with dance music masterminds Nile Rogers and Bernard Edwards (of Chic) that the funky femme four would become overnight sensations. Their first hit, "He's the Greatest Dancer" (1979), was a literal sketch of the quintessential narcissistic disco male—"Halston, Gucci, Fiorucci!"—which still works today (just ask Will Smith, who sampled the hook and was "Gettin' Jiggy Wit It" in 1998). The hypnotic cut "Lost in Music" is a personal fave. However, it was the release of "We Are Family" that guaranteed the women a place on infinity's playlist of dance songs. The groovy, hand-clapping anthem was used to rally everyone from baseball champions (Pittsburgh Pirates) to gay and, of course, lesbian groups. (Remarkably, for all its popularity the song missed the number one spot on the Hot 100 chart landing just under at number two.) Today, they are only a threesome—sister Kathy went solo—who continue to enliven crowds eager to boogie the night away. (candid of the Sledge sisters, c. 1979. Gary Gershoff/Retna)

dancing queen

Since **Grace Jones** (b. Grace Mendoza, 5/19/48, Spanish-town, Jamaica) first found fame as a runway model—what a sensation she must have been on the catwalk!—she appropriately titled her first album *Portfolio* in 1977. Two selections from that release, "I Need a Man" and "La Vie en Rose" (an excellent dance cover of the Piaf classic), were big disco hits (particularly among gay men). The albums *Fame* and *Muse* followed in 1978 and 1979, as did her growing number of fans and her reputation for stunningly visual, oftentimes blatantly sexual, performances. Certainly, no one else sounded or looked anything like Jones. In 1980, fully aware of a disco backlash, Jones released *Warm Leatherette*, a unique fusion of rock, soul, new wave, and dance. At the same time, her professional and personal relationship with artist Jean-Paul Goude resulted in the androgynous imagery that would become her most powerful and long-lasting look. Her next album, 1981's *Nightclubbing*, with its emphasis on reggae, yielded her biggest success, the marvelously raunchy "Pull up to the Bumper" (followed by the equally debauched "Nipple to the Bottle"). Though Jones had two more big dance hits in later years, "Slave to the Rhythm" and "I'm Not Perfect (But I'm Perfect for You)"—where does she come up with these great titles?!—she has never enjoyed mainstream success. Given the highly suggestive nature of her work, this would have been all but impossible. Undoubtedly, this lack of commercial viability is what has made her so attractive to "fringe" audiences. (candid of Jones in performance, c. 1978. Michael Ochs Archives)

Donna Summer (b. LaDonna Andrea Gaines, 12/31/48, Brookline, Mass.) worked her way up the ranks first in Europe, gaining recognition in a German production of the musical *Hair*. Then, in the mid-seventies, under the guidance of producers Pete Bellotte and Giorgio Moroder, the three created the revolutionary dance composition "Love to Love You Baby." Originally timed at sixteen-plus minutes (for easy play in discotheques), it was shortened by Neil Bogart (of Casablanca Records) for play on American radio. Tame by today's loosened moral standards, the then-provocative "orgasmic" voiceovers and throbbing synthesized beat created shock waves among listeners—and the world of popular music would never be quite the same place. A long succession of dance hits followed, with some more suited to clubland (the epic "Four Seasons of Love"), while others struck gold both on and off the dance floor: "I Feel Love," "MacArthur Park," "Heaven Knows," et al. Her hits "Hot Stuff" and "Bad Girls" (which has one of the most memorable hooks in music—"toot, toot, hey, beep, beep") successfully meshed disco with rock—giving Summer more "respectability" among contemporaries. She also scored a major triumph with the Oscar-winning "Last Dance" (from the film *Thank God It's Friday*, 1978), which is still a final-call favorite in clubs worldwide. Decades after she started, Summer still "works hard for the money" and is going strong—much to the consternation of those who bellowed "death to disco." (Unfortunately, she is one of the few dance artists who can say her career has survived intact.) Nevertheless, Summer—who is also an accomplished painter—is tired of the title "queen of disco," which she feels sets limitations on her work. One would be inclined to agree. Her songs are considered among the best examples of the dance genre, but her longevity owes just as much to well-crafted productions and an amazingly strong voice (that has not diminished over the years) as it does to a memorable beat. A five-time Grammy winner, Summer (her surname is an anglicized version of the last name she kept from her first husband, Herbert Sommer) gave fans the perfect line with the title of her most recent hit, "I Will Go with You"—and we certainly will! (Michael Ochs Archives)

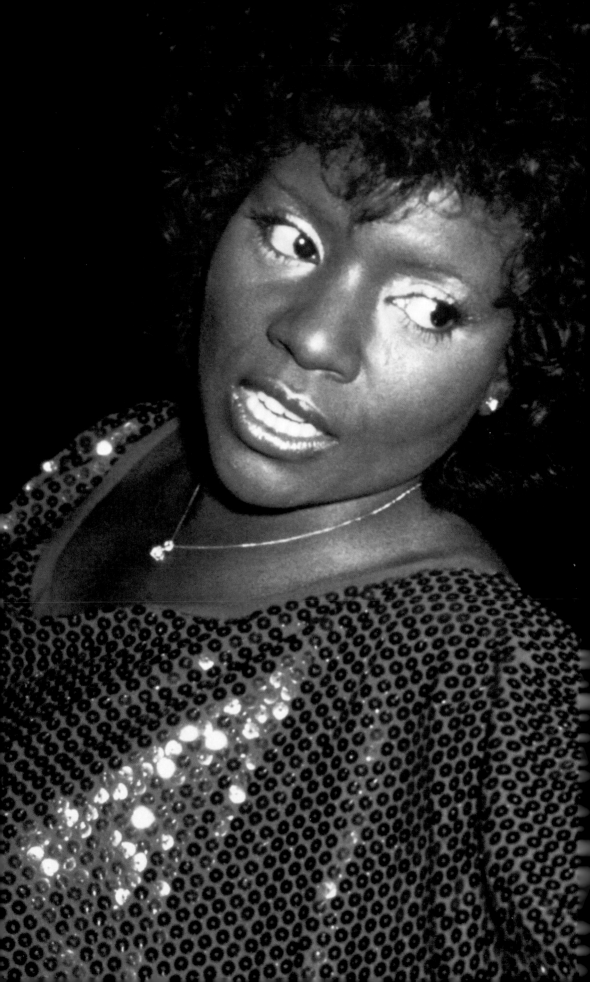

this spread: **Gloria Gaynor** (b. 9/7/49, Newark, N.J.) gave the women of the world (as well as a few good men) the eponymous dance smash "I Will Survive." For Gaynor, this was the perfect cap to a long and hard ride to the top that began in the mid-sixties. Even though she was "discovered" by music impresario Clive Davis, it wasn't until she teamed with Meco Monardo (the man responsible for the kitschy dance hit "Theme from Star Wars") that she found just the right rhythm to match her bluesy voice. The result was "Never Can Say Goodbye," considered one of the first disco crossover hits (and the first to be worked into an extended mix for club play). But that was in 1974! Five more years would still need to go by before proclaiming "I Will Survive," which was on top of almost every pop music chart in the world. In 1980, she received the first—and only—Grammy for Best Disco Recording (it has since been reestablished as Best Dance Recording) and recently the song was named by *Billboard* as the top dance hit of the twentieth century. Gaynor recently had another number-one dance hit—"Just Keep Thinkin' about You." What a survivor! (By the way, dear readers, no one fits the mold of gay-friendly disco "queen" better than Gloria Gaynor. Just a listen to the lyrics—yes, dance songs have lyrics!—of her big hits should help you understand how they dramatize a gay man's perspective of his world. Admittedly a tad exaggerated, but that is part of the allure.) (candid of Gaynor, c. 1979. Michael Ochs Archives)

inset: Any cut by **Linda Clifford** (b. 1944, Brooklyn, N.Y.) was sure to be a boogie-night favorite, and her priceless "If My Friends Could See Me Now" (from *Sweet Charity*) is one of the best dance remakes of a nondisco song ever recorded (a late-seventies music trend that had more misses than hits). Unfortunately, this former Miss New York State Beauty Queen only once emerged from behind closed disco doors: when her saucy "Runaway Love" became an outside chart hit. The song was also a trendsetter; Clifford's running, often spoken dialogue about the trials and tribulations of a contemporary black female became a "gimmick" used by many female R&B artists who followed. (album, *If My Friends Could See Me Now*) *inset:* Musically, Gloria Gaynor was hardly the first woman to declare her independence. An earlier example is **Helen Reddy** (b. 10/25/41, Melbourne, Australia). While her music doesn't hit the same primal notes as a dance artist's, she certainly struck a few chords when she penned "I Am Woman." Nonetheless, the road to the top for this 1972 emblem of the feminist movement was rocky. An original version was included in the soundtrack of the 1971 film *Stand Up and Be Counted.* Based on the mild strength of the movie's popularity, the song was reworked—adding a female chorus—and released as a single. Unfortunately, it stalled on the charts. But Reddy was eager for stardom and hit the pavement to promote her little-heard single. The strategy worked: Reddy earned a number-one hit and a Grammy for Best Pop Female Performance (for which she thanked God "because she makes everything possible"). A slew of hits followed, as well as a foray into films (with tepid results) and the stage (with a much better reception). If she has to, that Reddy can do anything! (candid of Reddy in performance, c. 1975. Michael Ochs Archives)

this spread: As the seventies slammed head on into the eighties, music did one of its familiar about-faces. Marching forward with the independence gained from "I Am Woman" and "I Will Survive," our feet seemed to get stuck in the gooey sentiment of the 1981 hit "Morning Train" (switched from its original title "Nine to Five," to avoid confusion with the Dolly Parton release). Fortunately, chirpy **Sheena Easton** (b. 4/27/59, Belshill, Scotland) broadened her appeal with songs like the Bond opus, "For Your Eyes Only," and the highly provocative duo of "Strut" and "Sugar Walls" (a song so rife with sexual entendre that moralists had a field day). Her relationship with the composer of "Walls," Prince, also resulted in her doing double duty on his song "U Got the Look." Easton's last big hit was "The Lover in Me" (1988), but no need to worry: she is still, reportedly, quite wealthy. Easton's a Grammy winner for Best New Artist (1981) and for her 1985 Spanish duet with Luis Miguel. (candid of Easton in performance, c. 1985. Chris Walter/Retna)

the woman in me

inset: In the early eighties, "disco" was considered a bad word, so dance music moved back underground (from where it came) to cultivate a fresher sound incorporating elements of punk, new wave, and electronica. (At the time, I was preparing for my own transition: a move from my hometown of Cincinnati, Ohio, to attend school in New York City.) Enter the duo, Yazoo. Two of their songs, "Don't Go" and "Situation," were a sensation; the perfect blends of old with new. But what made them most memorable (at least for me) were the lead vocals. Much to everyone's chagrin, what had sounded like a man's bluesy growl was actually coming from a woman, **Alison Moyet** (b. 6/18/61, Basildon, England). Moyet left Yazoo to pursue a solo career in 1983 and released the highly praised album *Alf*. Her amazing voice was perfect for the breakout hits "Invisible" and "All Cried Out." For a while she abandoned pop for jazz, which was thought to be a better showcase for her talents, but returned to pop in the late eighties. However, Moyet never enjoyed the same popularity in America as she did in England. Maybe she was just too hard to pin down. (Whatever the reason, her music played an important part in my life.) (portrait of Moyet, c. 1984. Adrian Boot/Retna)

this spread: By the middle to late eighties, dance music had fully resurfaced (although, honestly, it never went away), and there was no better example of this than in the career of **Jody Watley** (b. 1/30/59, Chicago). A former Soul Train dancer and member of the disco group Shalamar, Watley took a very serviceable voice, dance training, exotic looks, and a great sense of style to sashay her way to the top. (Personally, I was going through a lonely period in which I missed my hometown gang and was in desperate need for a pick-me-up; Watley's music and a great, new best friend—who liked to club hop—was just what the doctor ordered!) A Grammy winner as Best New Artist of 1987, Watley incorporated hip-hop and rap into her work and the resulting hits, including "Looking for a New Love," "Real Love," and "Friends," were successful forerunners of the tribalesque dance sounds of the last decade. She was also one of the first contemporary soul/dance artists to have her songs remixed for the growing house movement. (portrait of Watley, c. 1988. Adrian Buckmaster/Retna)

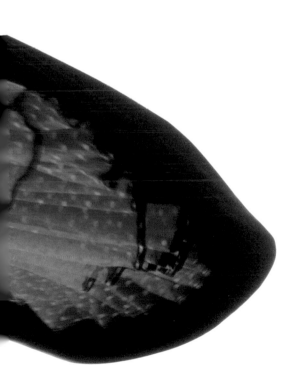

this spread: When the song "Foolish Beat" topped the charts in the Spring of 1988, seventeen-year-old **Deborah (Debbie) Gibson** (b. 8/31/70, Long Island, N.Y.) entered the history books as the youngest artist to sing, write, *and* produce a number-one song. However, by this time, having played the piano since age five and having written music since age six, she was more than likely used to the attention. Unfortunately, as is often the case when one reaches the top too quickly, there was no place to go but down. Especially for a teenager, it would be nearly impossible to sustain the momentum, let alone hold an audience ready to move on to the next fad or fashion. But Gibson had remarkable success—and *has* enough talent to forge ahead: as a stage performer, television producer and star, and more mature musical artist. (portrait of Gibson, c. 1986. Adrian Buckmaster/Retna)

inset: Okay, I'll admit that I put Gibson with **Bananarama** (Keren Woodward, b. 4/2/61, Bristol, England; Sarah Dallin, b. 12/17/61, Bristol, England; Siobhan Fahey, b. 9/10/58, Dublin, Ireland) because their outfits worked together. But they were contemporaries of each other, too, and both eschewed the overt sexuality prevalent in other acts. "Cruel Summer" was the trio's first big American hit (they were always more successful in their homeland, England), which was topped a couple years later by "Venus" and "I Heard a Rumour." In videos, they were known for their slightly amateurish choreography—and cute male dancers!—and came off as rather wholesome. Original member Fahey left in 1987, married Eurythmics member Dave Stewart, then founded the group Shakespear's Sister. Bananarama officially disbanded in 1993. (In case you were wondering, the name Bananarama is a combination of the children's show *The Banana Splits* and the Roxy music song "Pyjamarama." Go figure!) (candid of Bananarama, c. 1988. Adrian Boot/Retna)

As part of Eurythmics, a mesmerizing **Annie Lennox** (b. 12/25/54, Aberdeen, Scotland) had been widely perceived as only the frontperson for partner Dave Stewart's ingenious music. In actuality, she was often the lyricist and a full collaborator. But her contribution was constantly overshadowed by Stewart's lush orchestrations—and Lennox's own inventive visual artistry. All that would change when the duo split in 1989, and Lennox went on to a solo career. The successful release of the single "Why" and the album *Diva* in 1992 established Lennox as a singer/songwriter of the highest order, alongside Carole King and Joni Mitchell. *Diva* also turned out to be a far bigger success than anything previously done by Eurythmics, and Lennox went on to win a Grammy for the accompanying long-form video. Her followup, *Medusa*, was a cleverly conceived album of songs previously recorded by male vocalists. It met with equal praise and sales. Lennox's recent successes are noteworthy because they dispense with the notion that women musicians are "finished" when they hit middle age. Audiences both young and old interested in intelligently written, produced, and performed music know where to find it. (candid of Lennox in performance, c. 1990. Michael Putland/Retna)

this spread: Entertaining large audiences comes as nothing new to **Celine Dion** (b. 3/30/68, Charlemagne, Canada) who was the youngest of fourteen children. Heralded by many today as the new Streisand, Dion performed in her teens with her siblings until an introduction to local music manager Rene Angelil changed everything. Within a year, Angelil let go of all his other clients and mortgaged his home to finance Dion's first album. The gamble worked, and she had a succession of hit releases—but only in Canada! For real success she needed access to the lucrative American market—which meant Dion would have to learn English. It took over a year, but an earnestness the world would come to know—and love—paid off; in 1990, she made her English-language debut and began her meteoric ascent to the top. "Where Does My Heart Beat Now" was her first big single, followed by the "(Theme from) Beauty and the Beast" (an Oscar and Grammy winner), and "The Power of Love." Despite the marathon playing of her chest-thumping juggernaut "My Heart Will Go On" (from the 1997 film *Titanic*), Dion's most successful single is "Because You Loved Me" (from the 1996 film *Up Close and Personal*) —which logged six weeks at number one and an astounding all-time record of nineteen weeks atop the adult contemporary chart. Recently, Dion took the surprise step of retiring from show business at the peak of her fame. Whether this turn away from the industry to have children and tend to an ailing Angelil (whom she married despite his being nearly thirty years older) will hold, only time will tell. (Kevyn Aucoin)

inset: Wearing her trademark wide-rimmed black glasses, **Nana Mouskouri** (b. 10/15/36, Athens, Greece) has been singing for over forty years, recorded hundreds and sold hundreds of millions of albums, and collaborated with Quincy Jones and Harry Belafonte (whom she toured the world with). But "The White Rose of Athens" is still relatively unheard of on these shores—especially with today's listeners. Why? Because, surprise! English is not her first language. So, success in America on the same scale with which she has conquered the world has eluded her. Nevertheless, she is a huge favorite in Greece, France, Spain, and Germany—where she sings in their native tongues as well as the Orient. Famous for her renditions of "classical" music, "Ave Maria" is a great example of the sweet and clear singing that has won hearts the world over, but not here. (album, *Nana*, Fontana)

Nana

NANA MOUSKOURI
SINGS
Arranged & Conducted
by Bobby Scott

117

pop tarts

this spread: The word "pop" is a truncated form of the word popular. So wouldn't any musician categorized as such be a happy camper? Unfortunately, pop artists are often dismissed as intentionally mediocre, wholly derivative, and unoriginal. Ouch! that hurts (but obviously not enough to stem the flow). From her earliest days appearing in New York clubs (a gig at Danceteria was one that this author was lucky enough to witness!), **Madonna** (b. Madonna Louise Veronica Ciccone, 8/16/58, Bay City, Mich.) knew that false modesty was not likely to give her the superstardom she so earnestly wanted—or arguably deserved. So it quickly became apparent that she should toot her own horn. Or in this case, parlay an astounding, chameleonlike ability to refashion her musical output—with time out to marry, mother, and play movie actress—to reflect the passing fads and fashions of nearly two decades. (Can you believe it?!) From a simpleminded, move-your-booty perspective, has there been anything better to dance to than "Vogue" or "Music" (her twelfth number-one)? The "material girl"—who was once a cheerleader, studied piano, performed as a member of the Alvin Ailey dance troupe, and worked in a doughnut shop—is now one of the most successful singer/songwriter/producers of all time. (candid of Madonna, 1979. Archive)

inset: Pop princess **Britney Spears** (b. 12/2/81, Kentwood, La.) is part of a very long daisy chain of teenaged women who, over the years, have taken their place among music royalty. At age eleven, though initially thought too young, Spears successfully joined the cast of Disney's "Mickey Mouse Club" (which at one time also featured Spears's beau Justin Timberlake, of N-Sync, and rival Christina Aguilera). At the ripe old age of seventeen, she careened onto the top of the charts with "Baby, One More Time," followed closely by a succession of similar sounding ditties. Not surprisingly, she (along with Madonna) has become a role model for her throngs of youthful followers despite (or more likely because of) her unabashed attitudes about sex and sexuality—including her notorious "underwear" cover for the magazine *Rolling Stone* in 1999. No surprise too, that both singers have endured harsh criticism from concerned "adults" who are used to the more demure stances fancied by idols of their own youth. (candid of Spears signing autographs, 1999. Bill Davila/Retna)

this spread: One of the first performers to appear on the 1957 network debut broadcast of Dick Clark's highly influential talent showcase *American Bandstand*, **Connie Francis** (b. Concetta Rosa Maria Franconero, 12/12/38, Newark, N.J.) became a pop princess long before the title was overused. Beginning with "Who's Sorry Now" (1958)—a remake of a 1923 hit—to "Where the Boys Are" (a personal fave) and "Vacation" (1962), she had a string of top-10 hits a mile long and sold tens of millions of records—until her rule came to an end in the mid-sixties. Francis, who was then only in her mid-twenties, was never able to wear the crown again despite attempts to stay viable in the increasingly popular adult contemporary market. By the mid-seventies, after surviving a horrific assault, Francis went into seclusion; however, she has since resurfaced and appears on occasion to please her many nostalgia-hungry fans. (candid of Francis, c. 1960. Corbis-Bettmann)

inset: When young **Teresa Brewer** (b. Theresa Breuer, 5/7/31, Toledo, Ohio) had a hit with the song "Music, Music, Music" in 1949, she arguably became the first teen female star of the modern rock era. Of course, her career has long since been eclipsed by a succession of talented young women, but Brewer's success was also remarkable in that she appealed both to young *and* old audiences—as was evident in the popularity of her next big hit, "Til I Waltz Again with You" (1952). This was largely due to the fact that her voice made her sound much older than she actually was. However, by the mid-fifties, when true rock and roll began to make inroads, Brewer, only in her mid-twenties (like Francis), was already deemed too "long in tooth" for the fast encroaching throngs of screaming baby-boomer youths. But what does one do when the majority of your life lays ahead of you? In Brewer's case, she left to raise a family, then returned to music but devoted her time mainly to jazz music, where she has enjoyed a successful second career. (album, *For Teenagers in Love*, Coral, 1957)

country girl

this spread: The story goes that the song "Blue" was originally written for the legendary Patsy Cline, but the singer
died before she was able to make a recording; some forty
years later the soaring melody saw the light of day with wun-
derkind **LeAnn Rimes** (b. 8/28/82, Jackson, Miss.) Singing
since she was six, Rimes did not consider herself an
overnight sensation when she earned the distinction of being
the youngest performer to be awarded the Grammy for Best
New Artist (1996). The following year she had even more
crossover success with the release of the single "How Do I
Live." Though Rime's version far and away bested that of fellow country artist Trisha Yearwood's in both sales and rank-
ings, she would lose the Grammy to "veteran" Yearwood for
Best Country Female Vocal. Having crossed over from country to pop with no trouble, Rimes now faces the most daunt-
ing task of them all: keeping her amazingly successful
career alive into full adulthood. (portrait of Rimes, 1999.
Ross Pelton/Retna)

inset: When a thirteen-year-old LeAnn
Rimes hit big with "Blue," she was car-
rying on a tradition that had begun
decades before with the country-tinged
tunes of "Little Miss Dynamite" herself,
Brenda Lee (b. Brenda Mae Tarpley,
12/11/44, Lithonia, Ga.). Lee's extreme
youth, coupled with a surprisingly adult
voice, went beyond simple novelty; her
familiar hits "I'm Sorry," "I Want to Be Wanted," "Rockin' around the Christmas Tree,"
and "All Alone Am I" were all released before
she was twenty, but they contain a surprising
amount of mature sentiment that made them
appealing to all ages of listeners. Here's a bit of irony: Lee's
hit "All Alone Am I" was originally part of the soundtrack for
the 1961 film *Never on Sunday*, but because of its adult
theme a then-teenaged Lee was not able to view the movie
until years later. When music tastes changed, yet again, in
the mid-sixties, Lee went into semi-retirement, resurfacing in
the seventies as a full-fledged country artist, where she
remains today. (album, *Emotions*, Decca)

STEREO

Emotions

BRENDA
LEE

DECCA
RECORDS

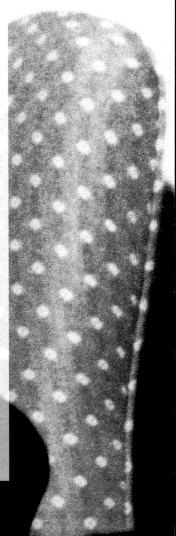

this spread: In homage to Patsy Cline—to whom her voice has often been compared—**k.d. lang** (b. Kathryn Dawn Lang, 11/2/61, Consort, Canada) called her early nineties backup group the Reclines. Initially lang dismissed "true" country music as corny (what a shock!) and instead developed her own style, which has been described as "torch and twang" or new tradition. She first encountered hesitancy at country radio because of her appearance and sexual ambiguity. They warmed up to her with the release of "Crying," a duet with the great Roy Orbison, which went on to win a Grammy. Her big coming-out (so to speak) occurred when she was chosen as the first person to grace the cover of *Entertainment Weekly* magazine with its premier issue in 1990; she disclosed her lesbianism to *USA Today* in 1992. That same year she released the album *Ingenue*, containing another Grammy-winning single "Constant Craving," and officially crossed over into pop, but she prefers to call this style "nouveau easy listening." (candid of lang, c. 1992. Valerie Phillips/Retna)

inset: Superlative vocal skills (with a voice that "boomed like Kate Smith's"), an outstanding songbook (which many have tried to replicate), and a tragically short life (she died at age thirty in a plane crash) all conspired to make **Patsy Cline** (b. Virginia Patterson Hensley, 9/8/32, Gore, Va.; d. 3/5/63) one of the few true legends in recorded music. Despite all this, Cline did not enjoy the unquestioned crossover success into pop as one would assume for such a revered artist—and she was not particularly keen on recording her first big hit, "Walkin' after Midnight" (claiming it was "nothing but a little old pop song"!). Nevertheless, at heart she remained and flourished as a country (and western) performer—becoming the first female artist to headline on tour—and her music still made its way onto turntables and pop playlists all over the world, then *and* now. Amazingly, her most beloved song, "Crazy" (written by Willie Nelson), did not go to the top of the country music chart, but her popularity remained indisputable: Cline's *Greatest Hits* album logged four years at number one and thirteen years total on *Billboard*'s back-catalog country list. A Grammy Lifetime Achievement award winner in 1995, Cline was the subject of the film *Sweet Dreams* (1985), starring Jessica Lange in the Oscar-nominated lead role (with her singing dubbed with Cline's recordings). At age four, Cline taught herself to dance and won a talent contest for her efforts. Where would we be now if she had decided to stay dancing? (album, *Sentimentally Yours*, Decca, 1962)

inset: **Crystal Gayle** (b. Brenda Gail Webb, 1/9/51, Paintsville, Ky.) was influenced by the work of pop artists like the Beatles, and her voice was well suited to torchy ballads. At the start of her career, she toured with her sister, Loretta Lynn. Not surprisingly, working this close just made Gayle sound too much like her sibling; she needed to go out on her own. The new Gayle was sophisticated, sexy, and nothing that music (country or pop) had ever seen. With songwriter Richard Leigh, she released the jazzy "Don't It Make My Brown Eyes Blue" in 1977. The song won two Grammy awards and the album, *We Must Believe in Magic*, became the first by a female country artist to sell over a million copies. Resplendent in her long, long hair (grown to three inches from the floor), Gayle followed up with a ton of crossover hits. Today, the lady whose first name came from sister Loretta (so the story goes) when she spotted Krystal's, a southern restaurant chain, keeps a lower profile and runs a store that sells—what else?—crystal! (album, *Hollywood, Tennessee*, Columbia, 1981)

this spread: After reading a couple of country-music biographies you begin to understand why Hollywood thought of them as perfect film material. Case in point: no fiction writer could come up with a better story than that of **Loretta Lynn** (b. Loretta Webb, 4/14/35, Butcher Hollow, Ky.) Raised in a shack during the years of the Depression, she was the second of eight children (and named after movie star Loretta Young). Married at thirteen, she had four children and many miscarriages before turning eighteen. She had six children in total and was a grandmother by age twenty-nine. Her husband, Oliver Vanetta Lynn (whose nickname "Mooney" was short for moonshine!), was an avid supporter of Lynn's work and helped to promote her in the early years. They had been together for forty-eight years when he passed away in 1996. (Legendary Patsy Cline was also a fan and advocate.) Lynn's mid-sixties classic, "Don't Come Home a' Drinkin (with Lovin on Your Mind)" came from the first album certified gold for a female country artist. Another hit, 1971's "Coal Miner's Daughter" became her best-loved song and the title of Lynn's now-famous autobiography. (The 1980 film version won an Oscar for actress Sissy Spacek.) Lynn was also the first woman named entertainer of the year by the CMA (Country Music Association) and country music's first millionaire. (portrait of Lynn, c. 1973. Bud Gray/MPTV)

this spread: The life story of legendary **Tammy Wynette** (b. Virginia Wynette Pugh, 5/5/42, Itawamba County, Miss.; d. 4/6/98)—dubbed the "First Lady of Country Music"—reads like the lyrics of one of her songs. Growing up poor, she worked as a cotton picker, beautician, waitress, and shoe-factory employee before fame knocked on her door. (Even after it did, she always kept a bowl of cotton in her house to remind her of her humble beginnings—and made sure her beautician's license was up-to-date, thinking "she could always go back"!) As a teen, she married a man who was almost always unemployed, had two children, and found herself forced to live in an abandoned log cabin. A third child almost died in infancy, during which time Wynette was working ten-hour days and rising at four to sing on a local radio show. By the mid-sixties, with her troubled marriage ended, she was fed up with her life and set about to make a change. Moving to Nashville, she auditioned for several labels until Epic signed her to a contract. Her record producer, Bill Sherrill, noticed that her ponytail hairstyle made her look "like a Tammy"—and the name stuck. Quickly going from country girl to superstar, her first dozen albums all went to number one, and her signature song, "Stand by Your Man"—among thirty-five number ones—became the biggest-selling single in country music history. Her biggest crossover hit? Surprisingly, "Justified and Ancient," her 1992 duet with the English group KLF. (Michael Ochs Archives)

inset: **Shania Twain** (b. Eileen Edwards, 8/26/65, Windsor, Ontario) surely inherited some of Wynette's take-charge manner and has definitely given it a sexier edge, which has allowed her to infiltrate (and, at times, dominate) the pop market in a way no other country artist has ever done. Married to rock producer/songwriter Robert "Mutt" Lange (Def Leppard, Foreigner), Twain and her husband created the best-selling country album of all time, 1997's *Come on Over* (eighteen million copies sold, and counting). Even though the album was criticized for sublimating Twain's country roots in favor of splashy pop production, cuts like "You're Still the One" (which was also remixed into a dance hit) obviously retained enough of the right stuff to appease both country and pop fans. Pretty enough to be a Revlon spokesmodel, the woman voted by People for the Ethical Treatment of Animals (PETA) as the sexiest vegetarian once held a job as a tree planter. (candid of Twain, 1995. Bill Davila/Retna)

this spread: Believe me, I mean no disrespect, but do all country music legends start out poor? You tell me: when **Dolly Parton** (b. 1/19/46, Sevier County, Tenn.) was born—the fourth of twelve children—the doctor was paid in corn-meal. Learning to play the guitar at an early age to accompany her own singing, Parton had a minor hit with a song titled "Dumb Blonde." It caught the attention of Porter Waggoner, who was looking for woman singer to costar with him on his variety show. The television union lasted through eight years (1966–1974), many Parton hits (including the autobiographical "Coat of Many Colors"), and countless boxes of the dishwashing soap Duz (remember that?!). After parting company, perky Parton crossed over into the mainstream with the hit "Here You Come Again," and topped the charts with "9 to 5" (for which she received an Oscar nomination) and "Islands in the Stream," her Bee Gees–penned duet with Kenny Rogers. Parton also wrote and originally recorded the mammoth Whitney Houston hit, "I Will Always Love You." In 1986, she opened the amusement park Dollywood, nestled in the Smoky Mountains, where it is said she gainfully employs all her family members and friends. Parton has the dubious honor of having the first successfuly cloned animal, a sheep, named for her. It seems the scientists rather distastefully equated two of the same animals with Parton's notoriously large bosom. Boys will be boys! (candid of Parton, 1981. Nancy Barr/Retna)

FAITH HILL
BREATHE

inset: In the relative short time of seven years, **Faith Hill** (b. 9/21/67, Jackson, Miss.) has gone from obscurity to the new century's hottest female country artist, half of country's hottest couple (her hubby is studly Tim McGraw), and sales of over eleven million albums. Not bad for a woman who used to sell T-shirts to make ends meet. But here is something to ponder: would Hill be as popular today if she weren't so marketable? Possibly not. But I don't mean to take anything away from her singing or the merit of her songs. Hill is immensely talented and "This Kiss" and "Breathe" are excellent country crossover hits. But in this age of instant video stardom, it is hard to see past such a pretty package and into its contents. (album, *Breathe*, Warner Bros., 1999)

131

this spread: **Emmylou Harris** (b. 4/2/47, Birmingham, Ala.) started out as a folksinger in Greenwich Village (as so many others during the sixties had done) but was forced to return home (to her parent's home in Washington, D.C.) after her first marriage failed and left her a single mother. A recommendation to meet with great country/rock artist Gram Parsons set her back on track. The two formed a fruitful professional (and secretly personal) union and recorded three albums before Parsons's untimely drug-related death in 1973. Harris picked up where the two left off and forged ahead. For well over twenty years, she released a succession of critically acclaimed albums and became a music force revered by countless mainstream and country artists. Oddly, Harris never saw the same level of chart success visited upon those who credit her as a major influence. However, her specialty, concept work (wherein individual singles are less important than the album as a whole), explains why very few of her singles ever charted (and why so few songs were even released). Her most popular recording was the 1987 landmark album *Trio*, with Linda Ronstadt and Dolly Parton (the three had also worked together on Harris's only top-40 single, "Mr. Sandman"). Her latest, 2000's *Red Dirt Girl*, slightly shifts the focus from her voice and musicianship to her songwriting. Harris is the winner of ten Grammy Awards. (portrait of Harris, 1978. Ed Thrasher/MPTV)

inset: A singer/songwriter, **Melanie** (b. Melanie Safka, 2/3/47, Queens, N.Y.) became a surprise star at famed Woodstock. Her first hits, "Lay Down (Candles in the Rain)" and "What Have They Done to My Song, Ma?" reinforced the notion that she was a folk performer, although her smash "Brand New Key" owed much more to pop (and was, incidentally, the first single the author ever bought!). Unfortunately, even after forming her own record label, she did not have the staying power of other female singer/songwriters and her success lasted only a few short years. Regardless, she still performs today for audiences eager to recapture the last days of flower power and burning incense. (album, *Gather Me*, Neighborhood, 1971)

JOAN BAEZ
vol.2

inset: **Joan Baez** (b. 1/9/41, Staten Island, N.Y.) is the "queen" of folk, but I underplay the title because it is so inconsistent with this style of music (besides, shouldn't it be "first maiden" anyway?). Starting out in the East Coast club scene in the late fifties, she sang mostly traditional folk songs; as the civil rights movement took hold, she turned more to works of protest. By some accounts credited with "discovering" Bob Dylan (the "king" of folk), the two spoke for the youth culture through their introspective and thought-provoking music. In these formative years, Baez did not enjoy enormous chart success—although she likely didn't care for such obvious signs of commerciality—until the release of the single "The Night They Drove Ole Dixie Down," which went gold in 1971. However, more important than awards or accomplishments, this soprano was (and remains) music's foremost antiviolence and antiwar proponent. (album, *Joan Baez, Volume 2,* Vanguard, 1961)

this spread: Forty years after Baez, **Jewel** (b. Jewel Kilcher, 5/23/74, Payson, Utah) has been widely credited with reintroducing folk music to current audiences. However, where much of Baez's music was politically charged, Jewel's seems more poetic and romantic. These qualities, combined with astonishing beauty, have made her quite the sensation (especially to those expecting a folksinger to appear rather plain). But the road to success for Jewel has been an interesting and hard one: early in her career, she lived in a van to keep living costs down and subsisted on carrots and peanut butter. Performing in coffeehouses in southern California, Jewel finally caught the attention of record executives who whisked her off to New York. Her 1995 debut album, *Pieces of You,* became one of the biggest-selling records of all time: singles "You Were Meant for Me" and "Foolish Games" became chart hits, a rarity in this category of music. Jewel then turned her attention to writing poetry, and her first collection, *A Night Without Armor* (1998), became a surprise best-seller (books of poetry *rarely* sell in great numbers). Most recently, she has added acting to her growing resume, appearing in Ang Lee's *Ride with the Devil* (1999). In the tradition of folksingers of the past, she has aligned herself with humanitarian causes, forming her own Higher Ground for Humanity, an organization that promotes education and environmental awareness. (FYI: Jewel is a skilled yodeler, and she once sang with the rap group Le Creme under the name "Swiss Miss.") (Marcel Hartmann/Retna)

just plain folk

this spread: A young **Joni Mitchell** (b. Roberta Joan Anderson, 11/7/43, Fort McLeod, Canada) became involved with another student in art college, and the couple had a child. The two did not marry, and she was left a penniless mother. Desperate and unable to find work, Mitchell admits that she married Chuck Mitchell out of necessity. Even so, she was forced to give up her baby girl for adoption. These sad circumstances must have influenced her work, especially when you listen to lyrics like "it's love's illusions I recall, I really don't know love at all" from her best-known song "Both Sides Now." Like Joan Baez, Mitchell had limited chart success (especially when measured by today's inflated standards), but this has not lessened her impact on the music industry. She considers herself an album-oriented artist; each album is a complete statement. Single cuts convey only part of the message, and so Mitchell has said she is not interested in releasing singles from her compositions. (The albums *Blue* [1971] and *Turbulent Indigo* [1994] are much-lauded examples of her unique style.) Many mainstream artists acknowledge Mitchell's contribution by incorporating her work into their own—including Janet Jackson, who retooled Mitchell's jaunty eco-statement "Big Yellow Taxi" into her 1998 cut "Got Til It's Gone." Mitchell did have one big mid-seventies hit, when her serene "Help Me" went to number seven on the pop charts and number one on the adult contemporary listings—with her blessings! Mitchell is a multi-Grammy winner (including Best Pop Album for *Turbulent Indigo*) and a Rock and Roll Hall of Fame inductee (1995). (FYI: Mitchell learned how to play the ukelele with a self-teaching record.) (Michael Ochs Archives)

inset: One artist who benefited greatly from Joni Mitchell's compositional skills was **Judy Collins** (b. 5/1/39, Seattle, Wash.)—whom Mitchell idolized. Collins recorded "Both Sides Now," making it an International hit and herself a major star along with it. Though trained as a classical pianist and a songwriter, Collins's career always did better when she interpreted other people's work, such as Stephen Sondheim's "Send in the Clowns" and her million-selling version of "Amazing Grace." (album, *A Maid of Constant Sorrows*, Elektra 1961)

PANORAMIC STEREO
a maid of constant sorrow
JUDY COLLINS

this spread: When **Carly Simon** (b. 6/25/45, New York City) first started out, she performed in Greenwich Village nightspots, initially singing folk music with her sister, Lucy, under the name the Simon Sisters. After the two split, Simon went solo and concentrated on writing, resulting in her first two hits, "That's the Way I've Always Heard It Should Be" and "Anticipation" (yep, the same tune used for those ketchup commercials!). That same year, 1971, she won the Grammy for Best New Artist. Her most famous song, "You're So Vain," which topped the charts in 1972, still has listeners guessing the intended subject: Warren Beatty or Mick Jagger (who sang backup vocals). During this same time, Simon married adorable James Taylor and they were a favorite pair of the decade. The two often recorded with one another—"Mockingbird" and "You Belong to Me"—but by the time they divorced in 1983, Simon's career itself had gone through a major change. Discovering the merits (and money) in film compositions—okay! she didn't need the money; her father was founder of publishing giant Simon & Schuster—Simon wrote the lush and sexy "Nobody Does It Better" for the James Bond movie *The Spy Who Loved Me* (1977), followed by "Coming around Again" for *Heartburn* (1986), and "Let the River Run" for *Working Girl* (1989)— which snagged her an Oscar. (Michael Ochs Archives)

inset: Possibly more so than any other artist, **Carole King** (b. Carole Klein, 2/9/42, Brooklyn, N.Y.) changed how female musicians are viewed by the public and the industry. Prior to her 1971 release of the blockbuster album, *Tapestry,* women in music were often perceived as lesser contributors—in terms of writing, production, and performing—than their male counterparts. But even as a young teen, King was already proficient in songwriting and piano playing. When she met and married Gerry Goffin, the two formed an unstop- pable music alliance, composing classic pieces for Aretha Franklin ("Natural Woman"), the Shirelles ("Will You Still Love Me Tomorrow?"), Little Eva ("Loco-Motion"), and the Monkees ("Pleasant Valley Sunday"). When they separated in 1967, all eyes focused on King's career: would she survive without Gof- fin? Undeniably, yes. Her first solo effort, *Tapestry,* came along when it was time for women to gain greater recognition and acceptance, and eloquent selections like "It's Too Late," gave voice to those demands. She really made the "earth move" under our feet. (album, *Tapestry,* CBS, 1971)

this spread: An enigmatic **Kate Bush** (b. 7/30/58, Bexleyheath, England) has earned a reputation for ingenious and original music. Her distinctive vocals and unique orchestrations—try her 1978 debut album *Wuthering Heights*, based on the Brontë novel—place Bush's work in a class by itself. Although she has enjoyed enormous success on her native soil, Americans often find her music quirky. However, one single managed to make a run for it: "Running up That Hill" is a perfect example of Bush's complex artistry, but its success gave the false impression that her music was being accepted by the mainstream. It hasn't crossed over. Eccentric and notoriously shy of the public, Bush perhaps will never be fully understood. (Adrian Boot/Retna)

inset: At age six, **Tori Amos** (b. Myra Ellen Amos, 8/22/63, Newton, N.C.) was the youngest person admitted to study classical piano at the Peabody Institute at Baltimore's Johns Hopkins University, but a nonconformist attitude got her expelled at age thirteen. She called her first band YKant Tori Read, a jab at her conservatory years; her own first name came from an admirer who remarked she looked more like a "Tori" than an Ellen when she performed. Early in her career, Amos was compared to Kate Bush, but her work is just as original and in many ways far more accessible. But even Amos considers herself an acquired taste, less like "potato chips" and more like "anchovies." Sitting at the piano, simply dressed, her stage presence (touched with eroticism) allows intimacy with fans—and into her often highly introspective songs. Amos has taken personal tragedies—rape, abuse, and miscarriage—and set these incidents to music without undermining their import. Even the titles of her albums—*Little Earthquakes* (1992), *Under the Pink* (1994), and *From the Choirgirl Hotel* (1998)—sound playful but have a serious underlying edge. (candid of Amos in performance, c. 1995. Larry Busacca/Retna)

this spread: As a young gay teen, even I knew a "babe" when I saw one, and **Linda Ronstadt** (b. 7/15/46, Tucson, Ariz.) was a babe! Singing with the group Stone Poneys, she had a 1967 hit with "Different Drum" but quickly went solo in 1968. Her first two albums had a country flavor—which she never lost. They were followed by a milestone third release, the 1972 self-titled *Linda Ronstadt* (backed by musicians Don Henley, Glenn Frey, et al., who subsequently formed the band the Eagles) with a sound that came to be known as California rock. Ronstadt put her personal stamp on the category with the smash hit, "You're No Good" in 1975, and for the rest of that decade she pleased both country and rock fans with notable efficiency. Memorable singles include the down-home "When Will I Be Loved," the gutsy "Heat Wave," and the plaintive "Blue Bayou" (her biggest seller). She even managed to master soul with her marvelous "Ooh Baby Baby" in 1978. Personally, I feel her cover of the country and western song "Desperado" is one of the best pieces of music ever recorded. By the eighties, she had made an abrupt (and by all accounts intelligent) move to the stage (and film), in *Pirates of Penzance* (1980), and released a trio of albums—*What's New* (1983), *Lush Life* (1984), and *For Sentimental Reasons* (1986) (all produced by Nelson Riddle, who was responsible for many of Frank Sinatra's best recordings)—that showcased her lighter side. Amazingly, Ronstadt has successfully recorded light opera, country, Latin, rock and roll, standards, and soul—and has the awards to show for it. (Michael Ochs Archives)

inset: That **Rickie Lee Jones** (b. 11/8/54, Chicago) is a multiaward-winning, platinum-selling singer/songwriter is somewhat incongruous with her rebellious demeanor. Jones had been arrested, had run away from home, and was thrown out of at least three different schools before recording anything. She also had major rows with show producers, pulling out of concert dates when they didn't let her perform the pieces she wanted. Jones has been dropped by her label for lagging sales and has fallen off the radar more times than you can imagine, but she still rebounds to popular and critical acclaim. She refuses to allow her music to be easily classified: her first hit, "Chuck E's in Love," is folk/rock; she won a Grammy for the jazzy "Makin' Whoopee"; and her latest release, *It's Like This*, is traditional pop. (album, *Rickie Lee Jones*, Warner Bros., 1979)

rock-a-bye baby

this spread: During the first half of her career, **Bonnie Raitt** (b. 11/8/49, Burbank, Calif.) seemed to walk along the hardest path to fame. While her gutsy, blues-inspired work earned her a reputation as a talented performer, her rowdy nature combined with a serious drinking problem made it impossible for her output to be consistent and—that awful word—saleable. After fifteen years of steady releases, she was dropped by her label and suddenly found herself right back where she had started: at the beginning. But all was not lost. Sobered up and with a new label, she astounded herself as much as the buying public with the release of the album *Nick of Time*. Smoothing out some of her rough edges, this work—a skillfully crafted blend of country, rock, blues, and pop appealed to audiences of Raitt's own generation as well as to new converts. When it won the Grammy for Album of the Year in 1989—among three others that year—the entire industry cheered. Here was an artist who survived (and surpassed) the odds stacked against her. Her victory was for all those who could muster the courage (and talent) to outlast fads and fashions. Subsequent releases have fared almost as well: *Luck of the Draw* (1991) gave her three more Grammys and her first (and only) top-five hit, "Something to Talk About." *Longing in Their Hearts* won a 1994 Grammy for Best Pop Album. A Rock and Roll Hall of Fame inductee in 2000, Raitt is the daughter of Broadway performer John Raitt. (Michael Ochs Archives)

inset: Soon after **Melissa Etheridge** (b. 5/29/61, Leavenworth, Kans.) was given a guitar at age eight she started writing her own songs. Later, she attended music college in Boston and, at eighteen, moved to Los Angeles. By her late twenties, she had released her self-titled first album and was headed for superstardom. But along the way she had to fight a mighty battle: few felt that Etheridge's career could survive her coming-out. But it did. If anything, it thrived (as did all of us) because of her honesty and integrity. However, for a while there, Etheridge's personal exploits *almost* overshadowed some very excellent work—the 1994 single "Come to My Window," in particular. The public became fascinated with her marriage to Julie Cypher and the birth of their two children (thanks to a "donation" from rocker David Crosby). Such was her popularity that even fashion doyen Mr. Blackwell placed her on his "worst-dressed list." As if she cared. (candid of Etheridge, 2000. David Atlas/Retna)

this spread: Back in the seventies, it was still a novelty for women to perform rock and roll (hell, it still is!), so when sisters **Ann** (left, b. 6/19/51, San Diego) and **Nancy Wilson** (right, b. 3/16/54, San Francisco) took to the stage, Heart became a pioneering music group. Their big hits during this period, "Crazy on You," "Magic Man," and "Barracuda," are as powerful and distinctive as those released by any major all-male concern. Heart appeared destined for a long and fruitful career, but internal combustion almost squelched the group's fire when both sisters formed personal relationships with brothers, and backup support, Roger and Dave Fisher. When things soured, the Fishers departed. Regrouping, Heart was reinvigorated, and their biggest successes were still to come. A tad softer in tone than earlier pieces, "Tell It Like It Is," "What about Love?," "Never," "These Dreams," and "All I Wanna Do Is Make Love to You," became massive hits—even on the adult contemporary charts! Despite their longevity and remarkable output, the sisters have never won a Grammy award. But sister Nancy is married to Oscar-winning writer/director Cameron Crowe. (candid of Heart, c. 1975. Govert de Roos/Sunshine/Retna)

inset: I guess if I had to choose my favorite female rock star, I'd pick **Chrissie Hynde** (b. 9/17/51, Akron, Ohio) of the Pretenders. Though you would never call her delicate, there is something about her sweet, almost broken voice laid over a pulsing rhythmic track that makes her music quite irresistible. Maybe it's also because I personally feel that tracks like "Brass in Pocket" and "Don't Get Me Wrong" are far more enjoyable to listen to than the usual hypermasculine, grunting rock cuts. Whatever the reason, I am surely not alone. Hynde, who moved from the Heartland to start her career at the very epicenter of the punk movement—mid-seventies London—has also endured her share of great misfortunes: two founding members of the Pretenders both died of drug overdoses within a year of the band's initial success. Hynde forged ahead, and today she is a music icon *and* a passionate campaigner for animal and environmental rights. (FYI: my absolute favorite Hynde song: the sublimely transcendent "State of Independence." (album, *Pretenders*, Sire, 1980)

this spread: "Beauty and the beat" **Debbie Harry** (b. 7/1/45, Miami) and her group Blondie had been shuffling around for years before they let a little disco step into their lives. The subsequent single, "Heart of Glass," is hard to categorize; it is neither an all dance, rock, or new wave song, yet it utilizes the best features of all three. When released in 1979, it went straight to the top of the charts—and established the group as one of the preeminent music attractions on both sides of the Atlantic. Harry, a former beautician and Playboy bunny, became rock's reigning female sex symbol, but the notoriety (and founding member Chris Stein's illness) created problems among the group and they disbanded in 1982. However, during their short tenure, they did their best not to be boxed-in musically and were the first group to have a number-one reggae song, "The Tide Is High," as well as a song that featured rap, "Rapture." (They also had a purer, new wave dance hit with Giorgio Moroder's "Call Me" from the 1980 film *American Gigolo*.) When Blondie stopped recording, Harry continued as a solo act and appeared in a number of films, most memorably John Water's *Hairspray* (1988). More important, she stayed by boyfriend Chris Stein's side and nursed him back to health. By the late nineties, the group was reformed and recording together again. (Michael Ochs Archives)

inset: Every member of the group No Doubt is attractive, but whether it's because she sports hot-pink hair or face paint, **Gwen Stephani** (b. 10/3/69, Fullerton, Calif.) is the focus of attention. She went even so far as to solo on the cover of *SPIN* magazine in 1996. But fame and fortune were certainly no guarantee for her or the band when they started out. In 1991, when grunge music ruled the day, their self-titled first album received no airplay because it was deemed too upbeat. Three years later, *Tragic Kingdom* (1994) was released and initially fell flat. But by this time the shroud of angst-rock was being lifted away, and the group's tenacity paid off. The hit single "Don't Speak," originally written as a love song between members Stephani and Tony Kanal, shifted its focus as the two broke up before its release. (FYI: original founding member Eric Stephani, Gwen's brother, quit the group just prior to their breakthrough to work as an animator for *The Simpsons*.) (candid of Stephani, 1997. Steve Granitz/Retna)

this spread: The fickle nature of fame is such that a major success like **Pat Benatar** (*b.* Patricia Andrzejewski, 1/10/53, Lindenhurst, N.Y.) can be on top of the world one year and nowhere to be found the following. Though it may not have actually happened that precisely, it certainly seemed like it did. At her peak, Benatar won Grammy awards for Best Rock Female Performance four years in a row, released a succession of top-five albums (containing such hits as "Hit Me with Your Best Shot" and "We Belong"), was an MTV video mainstay (especially with "Love Is a Battlefield"), and was the unrivaled queen of early eighties rock. Nevertheless, by 1986, whether it was because music tastes had moved on or, more likely in Benatar's case, because she wanted to devote time to motherhood, the rocker dropped off the radar screen. Once a waitress and a bank clerk, this classically trained singer still records today. (candid of Benatar in performance, 1982. Richard Fuscia/Retna)

inset: Then there are artists like **Cyndi Lauper** (b. 6/20/53, Queens, N.Y.) who, despite enormous success, never get the respect they deserve. Often dismissed as more a visual curiosity than a music talent, Lauper wrote and performed a number of delightful pieces of pop rock that may well stand the test of time and prove her critics wrong. "Time after Time" and "True Colors" are moving and memorable ballads, and there is no quicker way to get an eighties-themed party started right than by turning on "Girls Just Wanna Have Fun" (from her multimillion-selling 1983 album *She's So Unusual,* which granted, she is!). As a teen, she hitchhiked cross-country with her dog, Sparkle, then returned home to study art before embarking on a musical career in 1974. Ten years later, she received the 1984 Grammy for Best New Artist. (candid of Lauper in performance, c. 1985. Adrian Boot/Retna)

151

inset: If the story of women in music is about diversity, humanity, and endurance, what better way to end *Songbird* than with the pairing of two of its most revered artists? Without question, the brief life and times of rock legend **Janis Joplin** (b. 1/19/43, Port Arthur, Tex.; d. 10/4/70) embodies the dark side of celebrity, but it is only one person's story. Whereas Joplin could not overcome pressures and survive, easily someone else might have. As a young woman, Joplin hitchhiked cross-country to San Francisco and insinuated herself into its burgeoning youth culture. Early inspirations were Bessie Smith (for whose grave Joplin, when she became successful, bought a headstone) and Odetta. Joplin showed a knack for blending blues with rock, and her whisky-soaked voice flowed perfectly over a three-octave range. But Joplin took to drugs as easily as she took to music and singing, becoming so rankled by her addiction that she never fully realized her potential while living. Her greatest triumph occurred posthumously, when "Me and Bobby McGee" went to number one. The single's success in many ways also signified an end to the freewheeling California hippy lifestyle that was her undoing. (candid of Joplin in performance, c. 1970. Baron Wolman/Retna)

this spread: **Tina Turner** (b. Anna Mae Bullock, 11/26/38, Brownsville, Tenn.) is part Native-, part African-American, all legend. Born to a family of sharecroppers, Turner moved to St. Louis in her teens to live with her mother. There, she fell in love with music and gave up early aspirations to become a nurse; she also met her husband-to-be, Ike, a gifted musician with a volatile temper. Their act, named the Ike and Tina Turner Revue, owed much of its success to Turner's energetic onstage performances (those legs! those moves!), and their biggest hit, "Proud Mary," is a rock classic. But fame did not sit well with Ike, and escalating abuse eventually caused his wife to, literally, run for her life. With only thirty-six cents and a gas credit card, Turner escaped his clutches only to find herself an unwanted, faded star. She forged ahead, and for nearly a decade played substandard gigs performing her old hits. A change of management sparked what was to become one of the greatest comebacks in music history. When "What's Love Got to Do with It," released in 1984, went to number one and won Turner three Grammy awards (including Record of the Year), no one was more humbled by the success—or more deserving. (candid of Turner in performance, c. 1971. Michael Ochs Archives)

There is no fair way to determine who may be the *best* female singer of all time, but there are ways to show who may have been the most popular at any one given time. With that in mind, I offer the following lists for your review. Information was compiled and combined from a variety of resources. I cannot vouch for their absolute accuracy.

THE 25 TOP FEMALE SINGERS

Based on a combination of sales, airplay, and length of stay on the charts, this list does not include artists whose majority of work was recorded prior to 1940 or after 1999. If it did, singer Ada Jones (who was enormously popular at the beginning of the twentieth century, but now forgotten) would become an overwhelming leader.

1. Mariah Carey
2. Madonna
3. The Andrews Sisters
4. Janet Jackson
5. Whitney Houston
6. Patti Page
7. The Supremes
8. Dinah Shore
9. Donna Summer
10. Olivia Newton-John
11. Karen Carpenter
12. TLC
13. Celine Dion
14. Barbra Streisand
15. Doris Day
16. Kay Starr
17. Monica (Arnold)
18. Diana Ross
19. Rosemary Clooney
20. Jo Stafford
21. Brandy
22. Margaret Whiting
23. Toni Braxton
24. Roberta Flack
25. Teresa Brewer

left: **Lola Falana** (b. 9/11/42, Philadelphia). This quintessential nightclub performer of the late sixties and seventies earned the nickname the "First Lady of Las Vegas" and was marvelously spoofed on the comedy SCTV as "Lola Heatherton." (candid of Falana in performance, 1979. Trindl/MPTV)

right: **Pearl Bailey** (b. 3/29/18, Newport News, Va.; d. 8/17/90) had a way of almost slurring the words in her songs (as in "Two to Tango") that was most appealing. (album, *The Intoxicating Pearl Bailey*, Mercury, 1958)

THE 25 TOP SONGS FROM THE LAST 25 YEARS

This listing is based on records performed by a *solo* female artist. Therefore, high-ranking songs from groups or duos involving men (Blondie, the Captain & Tennille, etc.) are not shown.

1976—"Love Hangover" (Diana Ross)
1977—"You Light Up My Life" (Debby Boone)**
1978—"MacArthur Park" (Donna Summer)
1979—"Bad Girls" (Donna Summer)
1980—"Upside Down" (Diana Ross)
1981—"Physical" (Olivia Newton-John)**
1982—"Mickey" (Toni Basil)
1983—"Flashdance . . . What a Feeling" (Irene Cara)
1984—"What's Love Got to Do with It" (Tina Turner)
1985—"Crazy for You" (Madonna)
1986—"Greatest Love of All" (Whitney Houston)
1987—"I Wanna Dance with Somebody" (Whitney Houston)
1988—"Anything for You" (Gloria Estefan)
1989—"Miss You Much" (Janet Jackson)
1990—"Nothing Compares 2 U" (Sinead O'Connor)
1991—"Rush, Rush" (Paula Abdul)
1992—"I Will Always Love You" (Whitney Houston)*
1993—"Dreamlover" (Mariah Carey)*
1994—"The Power of Love" (Celine Dion)
1995—"Fantasy" (Mariah Carey)
1996—"Unbreak My Heart" (Toni Braxton)
1997—"Wannabe" (Spice Girls)
1998—"The Boy Is Mine" (Brandy & Monica)*
1999—"If You Had My Love" (Jennifer Lopez)
2000—"Music" (Madonna)

*denotes a song that was the highest charter for that year
**denotes a song that was the highest charter of that decade

WOMAN TO WOMAN

Here are some pairings of female singers and groups whom I feel have something in common with one another. The connection may be the sound of a voice or the style of a look. In any case, there is no scientific process behind the choices.

Mariah Carey—Whitney Houston
Donna Summer—Irene Cara
Anastacia—Taylor Dayne
Macy Gray—Billie Holiday
Grace Jones—Sonique
Christina Aguilera—Britney Spears
The Supremes—Destiny's Child
Celine Dion—Barbra Streisand
Cher—Jennifer Lopez
Jill Scott—Odetta

intoxicating pearl bailey

THE AUTHOR'S 25 MUSIC RECOMMENDATIONS

The selections listed below are very personal so forgive me if some of the choices seem a bit unusual. This list, which is in no particular order, doesn't represent even a quarter of what I could suggest.

* *Doris Day: Greatest Hits*, Doris Day (Columbia, 1958): Yes, I know it's corny, but I'm that kinda guy. Besides, she's a girl from my hometown (Cincinnati), and you can't get a better feel for the fifties.

* *The Miseducation of Lauryn Hill*, Lauryn Hill (Ruffhouse/Columbia, 1998): A stunning collection by the finest new female vocalist in years that includes the most ingenious remake in a long time: "You're Just Too Good to Be True."

* *Funny Girl*, various (soundtrack, 1968): This was "Babs" at her absolute peak. Listen to "Don't Rain on My Parade" if you doubt me.

* "Music," Madonna (Maverick, 2000): An amazing swirl of percolating techno and proof that Madonna, even in her forties, can still get you groovin' and dancin' easier than anyone.

* "At Last," Etta James (Argo, 1961): If the word "swoon" did not exist, it certainly would have been invented after a listen to this song. (If hearing this too often in Starbucks has got you loopy, try Dinah Washington's "What a Difference a Day Makes.")

* *Janet*, Janet Jackson (Virgin, 1993): This album is so sexually sophisticated it feels like you're having a date with your CD player. It also has some of the best examples of sampling other artists' music.

* "Blue Bayou," Linda Ronstadt (Asylum, 1977): It's like being there, without the mosquitoes and alligators.

* "Old Cape Cod," Patti Page (Mercury, 1957): Okay, I'm partial to P'town, but this one could make anyone pine for an ocean breeze.

* "From This Moment On," Pat Suzuki (from the album *Broadway '59*, Mercury, 1959): The showstopping number from *Kiss Me Kate*, especially noteworthy when you realize the singer is Japanese-American.

* "I'm Looking for a New Love," Jody Watley (MCA, 1987): Even on my deathbed I'd wanna get up and dance to this one.

* "Sunny Came Home," Shawn Colvin (Columbia, 1997): Perhaps the best song from the recent music "folk wave."

* "Automatic," the Pointer Sisters (Planet, 1984): Back when techno wasn't even a word, let alone a sound (and flawless vocals).

* "I'll Get over You," Crystal Gayle (1976): Just about as simple a country gem as you can get.

* "I Will Always Love You," Whitney Houston (Arista, 1992): Yeah, I know, but try to remember when you first heard it.

* "Pull Up to the Bumper," Grace Jones (Island, 1981): This one makes you wanna do things you could never tell your mother about.

* *Donna Summer: Anthology*, Donna Summer (Mercury, 1993): An immaculate collection—but don't forget she's had a trio of big dance hits since.

* *The Very Best of Dionne Warwick*, Dionne Warwick (Rhino, 2000): Why bother choosing; they're all good.

* "Broken-hearted Melody," Sarah Vaughan (Mercury, 1959): With that voice, need I say more?

* *The Patsy Cline Collection*, Patsy Cline (box set, MCA, 1991): You'll go "crazy" over this one.

* "And I Am Telling You I'm Not Going," Jennifer Holiday (from the score of the 1981 Broadway show *Dreamgirls*): This could make anyone wanna play drag queen for "one night only."

* "The Man That Got Away," Judy Garland (Columbia, 1954): Did I mention that I was gay? Stupendous.

* "Where the Boys Are," Connie Francis (MGM, 1960): See above.

* "Love Hangover," Diana Ross (Motown, 1976): See above again, just add a pair of tight jeans.

* "Help Me," Joni Mitchell (Asylum, 1974): Who said pop commercialism and artistic integrity don't mix?

* *Medusa*, Annie Lennox (Arista, 1995): I know Lennox's earlier *Diva* got most of the praise, but this one is just so easy on the ears—and heart.

and one to grow on:
* "Un Bel Di," Leontyne Price (from the Puccini opera *Madame Butterfly*): You gotta get some culture somewhere!

left bottom: **Yma Sumac** (b. Emperatriz Chavarri, 9/10/27, Ichocan, Peru). Hoax or the real deal? Sumac had one of music's most curious careers. Alternating rumours surrounded her background: she was either an Incan princess or a Brooklyn housewife, Amy Camus (Yma Sumac spelled backwards). In any case, she was a popular novelty act, singing (and chirping) songs based on Peruvian folk songs. (album, *Legend of the Sun Virgin*, Capitol, 1951)

right: **Fran Jeffries** (b. 1939, San Jose, Calif.) was once married to singer Dick Haymes in the late fifties, and they often worked together in Las Vegas. But as a solo performer, Jeffries really knew how to strut her stuff. Catch her in a tight sweater singing "It Had Better Be Tonight" in the 1964 film *Pink Panther*. Jeffries was also married to director Richard Quine and still, on rare occasion, performs and records today. (Michael Ochs Archives)

well-charted

for the record

this spread: Literally, **Donna Loren** (b. 3/7/47) popped up in a handful of sixties beach movies; she was rarely onscreen longer than the length of a song! Her best recording, "It Only Hurts When I Cry" from *Beach Blanket Bingo* (1965), shows off a really great voice that went sorely underused. Loren was also the first, and only, "Dr. Pepper Girl"—a promotional stint that lasted five years in the mid-sixties. She and her image were used to sell the soda all across the country. Loren is now a fashion designer living in Hawaii. (film still from *Beach Blanket Bingo*, 1965. Michael Ochs Archives)

inset: Though never a major recording or film star, **Joey Heatherton** (b. 9/14/44, Rockville Center, N.Y.) managed to carve out a curious career filled with guest appearances and commercial endorsements: she appeared on the very first *Dean Martin Show* in 1965, among dozens of other television spots, and capitalized on her sex kitten image as a *purr*-veyor of mattresses for Serta. (candid of Heatherton, c. 1969. Everett)

I could go on singing, but the time has come for this song to end. On that note, I would like to offer thanks to the following individuals (it takes a lot of talent to make a "star" look good!) for their help, contributions, and support of this project:

To my editor, Chris Steighner, whose difference in age from myself (he's years younger!) only added to the scope of *Songbird*—and was a constant reminder that all gay men do not automatically or exclusively love movie musicals, torch singers, and disco. To everyone at **Universe** including Charles, Bonnie, John, and José: let the "record" state that your allowing me to play my own kinda music is gratifying and humbling, to say the least.

To my chorus of loved ones: Joe and Dan, Tony (my most musical friend, and I mean that in a nice way!), Miisa (just wait 'til you see my next one!), Lee and the kids, Teresa and Ward, Peter and John, Jim and Gary, Mark, Harris and Mitch (thanks for the recommendation!), Dan O., Darlene and John, Wayne, Joyce, and Vicky (I hope you like some of the choices!). To Jan, Tom, Prescott, Gordon, Dad and Len. To Mom, for deliberately (or not) subliminally directing me to singers of the fifties, then and now. To Mr. Beene, for kidding me about Doris Day all these years. To Kevyn, whose profound affection for many of the women in this book, manifested during our friendship together, eventually had its effect on me—thank you for perservering. To Red, for staring down at me from atop the computer—making sure I hit every note. And to Robert, especially, to whom I never sing enough praises—I know I can be a little sharp and a little flat at times, but you always put a song in my heart.

To the following individuals and organizations who also give a person something to sing about: Michael Thompson; Norman Curry and Donna Daley at **Corbis**; Glenn Bradie at **Everett**; the Mendelbaum Bros. at **Photofest**; Yen Graney at **MPTV**; Bob Cosenza, Margie Steinmann, and Phil Moad at **Kobal**; Jonathan, Helen, Larissa, and Laura at **Michael Ochs**; and my new cohort, Margaret at **Retna**. To all of you: THANKS!

this spread: Raised in Australia, as a young teen, **Olivia Newton-John** (b. 9/26/48, Cambridge, England) won two contests: the first, as "the girl who looked most like actress Hayley Mills," and the second, for a talent contest singing "Everything's Coming Up Roses." Newton-John's first American hit was the country song "Let Me Be There," and her biggest was "Physical," which revealed a sexier side to the rather wholesome singer. The single was also the eighties' most popular song. (candid of Newton-John being made up for a performance in 1979. Gunther/MPTV)

inset: Sweet and innocent **Jane Powell** (b. Suzanne Burce, 4/1/29, Portland, Ore.) was the singing girl next door who always had a smile on her face even when movie roles began to disappear. Two of her best film roles: *Seven Brides for Seven Brothers* and the unintentionally gay-friendly *Athena* (both 1954). (magazine, *Screen Album*, Summer, 1950)

closing page: **Bobbie Gentry** (b. Roberta Streeter, 7/27/44, Chickasaw County, Miss.) was the grooviest country chick ever, with her smash "Ode to Billie Joe" and mod wardrobe. She was also a 1967 Grammy winner for Best New Artist. (candid of Gentry, 1967. Gunther/MPTV)

back endpaper: The cultlike popularity of **Stevie Nicks** (b. 12/3/45, Phoenix, Ariz.) can be somewhat startling to the uninitiated, but not to those who appreciate her gifted songwriting and angelic, almost desperate vocals. Her successful fight against cocaine addiction and continual recording throughout has also earned her a music industry survivor "medal." Her finest composition for Fleetwood Mac?: "Dreams" or Rhiannon." Her finest solo effort? I'd pick "Stand Back" for its message, a throbbing underbeat, and a bevy of boppin' boys in the then relatively new medium of video. (candid of Nicks in performance with Fleetwood Mac, 1979. Mike Kagan/Retna)

back cover, clockwise from top left: **Vikki Carr** (b. Florencia Martinez Cardon, 7/19/41, El Paso, Tex.) was another early "Latin" singer who had a big hit with "It Must Be Him" in 1967. (album, *Anatomy of Love*, Liberty, 1965). **Sheryl Crow** (b. 2/11/63, Kennett, Miss.) is the thinking man's rock chick, or so she has been called. Winner of the Best New Artist Grammy in 1994, Crow had her biggest hit (to date) with "All I Wanna Do" (1994). (candid of Crow in performance, 1997. Steve Granitz/Retna). Beyond having a name that is hard to pronounce, **Björk** (b. Björk Gudmundsdottir, 11/21/65, Reykjavik) has a musical style that is hard to describe. She took her unique house sounds ("Human Behavior") around the world and to those in the know became the artist de rigueur. Lately, she turned to acting (*Dancing in the Dark*, 2000) and created quite a flutter when she appeared in a swan dress at the 2001 Oscar ceremony. (candid of Björk in performance, 1997. Jay Blakesburg/Retna) **Joni James** (b. Joan Carmello Babbo, 9/22/30, Chicago) was considered a fresh-faced, wholesome singer, whose biggest hit, "How Important Can It Be?" is, lyrically, a rather provocative tune. (album, *Je T'Aime . . . I Love You*, MGM). **Jaye P. Morgan** (b. Mary Margaret Morgan, 12/3/31, Mancos, Colo.) had a couple of big hits, including "That's All I Want from You" (1954), but is unfortunately remembered as a regular on TV's *The Gong Show*. (album, *Soft and Easy*, MGM). **Etta James** (b. Jamesetta Hawkins, 1/25/38, Los Angeles) struggled for years with a heroin addiction but continually recorded hits, including the sensational "At Last" (1961). (album, *The Second Time Around*, Chess, 1961)

NEW AUTOGRAPHED PORTRAITS PLUS INSIDE DATA ON 100 HOLLYWOOD STARS

SCREEN ALBUM

MAGAZINE

PUBLISHED SINCE 1935

SUMMER 15¢

DELL

TWO NEW ALBUM SPECIALS!
Complete picture life story of Joan Evans (p. 4)
A daily record of the lives of 300 stars (p. 46)

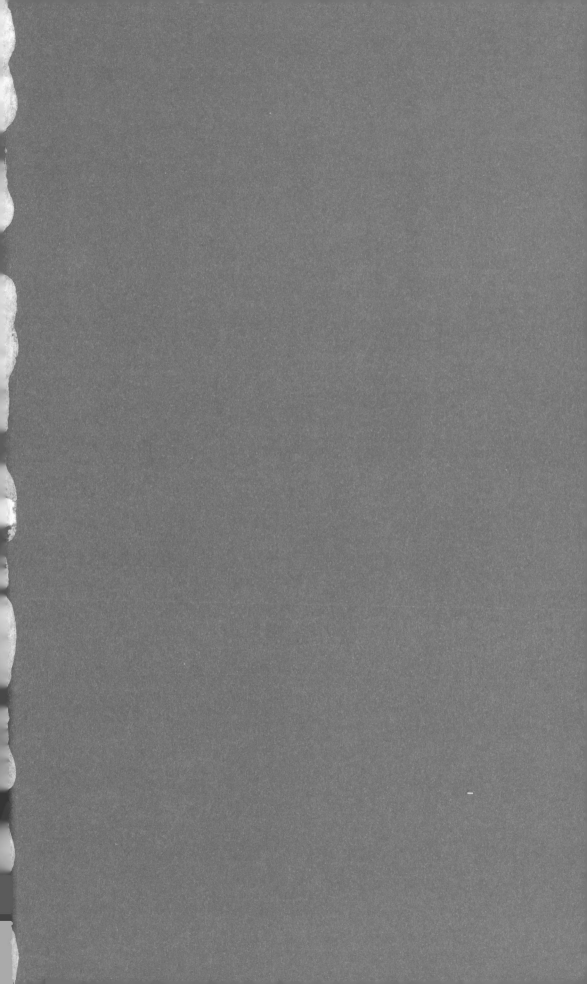